/

Stronger Than Hate

This story has been very important in our family life ... and we met the author: an amazing man.

We hope you'll like it too.

With thanks to you, for your companionship and guidance,

With friendship and love,

Valérie & Charles

Stronger Than Hate

Struggling to Forgive

by Tim Guénard

Translated by Michael Breck

Templegate Publishers
Springfield, Illinois

Originally published in French as *Plus fort que la haine* by
Les Presses de la Renaissance
12, Avenue d'Italie
75013 Paris - France

Templegate Publishers
302 East Adams Street
P.O. Box 5152
Springfield, Illinois 62705-5152
217-522-3353
templegate.com

ISBN 0-87243-262-9
Library of Congress Control Number 2003107782

Contents

Preface

It took me years of silence and love to write down nearly everything.

The events recounted in these pages are ones that I lived. This is not a novel. Please forgive my somewhat oral style; I'm not used to writing. I'd rather tell.

To protect certain people, I decided to change some names and places. That's the only twist in the truth I allowed myself to make. Please forgive me also for not being all that accurate when it comes to dates. I lived several lives at once. Sometimes the memories overlap. No matter. I am as old as my hope.

For propriety's sake, I've also kept to myself things of a strictly intimate nature that could not be made public.

I have kept quiet so as not to bind certain people to the pain they caused me. I don't want to keep them from changing. They have the right to surprise me.

I spoke out only after my father's death, out of respect for a man I wanted to kill, and learned to love even as he passed from this life.

Foreword

My life's story is as rough as my face.

My nose alone has been broken 27 times. Twenty-three of those were from boxing; four were from my father.

The most violent blows came from the one who should have taken me by the hand and said: "I love you."

He was Iroquois. When my mother left him, the poison of alcohol drove him crazy. He beat me to death even before my life could prolong the massacre.

I survived on the hope of three things: getting thrown out of the correctional home where I had been placed—a feat never before achieved—becoming a gang leader, and killing my father. I got around to all but the third, and that one came close.

For years I lived off the flame of revenge.

While in my prison of hate, I was visited by people filled with love; within my heart they brought me to my knees. I owe my life to the broken, distraught, handicapped and "abnormal" people whom our society has rejected. I also learned from them a tremendous lesson about love. I dedicate this book to them. It's through them that I was able to be reborn.

This unexpected encounter with love turned my whole world upside down.

Now I live in a big, bright house near Lourdes, with my wife, Martine, and our children, Églantine, Lionel, Kateri and Timothée, along with a few people just stopping in before going on their way.

This morning I set up my beehives on the mountainside. Tomorrow, I'll move them elsewhere, near other flowers, other aromas. I love the silence of the hills that whisk me off toward the horizon.

A bee flutters around me, buzzes around my face, then returns to a flower, laden with pollen. Its life is as metered as a musical score. It plays the notes of its lineage, the age-old orders of its genetic code. A bee, like any animal, is incapable of changing its programmed behavior.

Man can.

Man is capable of utterly changing his destiny for better or for worse.

I was an abandoned child, the son of an alcoholic, and I defeated my own fate. I showed up my genetic makeup. That's my pride. My name is Philippe, but people call me Tim because my Iroquois name is Timidy. It means "Lord of the Horses." My shattered memories were harder to tame than a wild thoroughbred.

Guénard can mean "Strong in Hope." I've always believed in miracles. I never lacked this hope, even in the darkest hours. I now want others to have it.

Like my Indian ancestors, I have no fear of heights. I fear only one abyss: the most frightening depth of self-hatred.

My only other fear is not to love enough.

Being a man takes balls. Being a man of love takes even bigger balls.

After years of struggle, I buried the hatchet with my father, with myself and with my past.

Every so often I get behind the wheel of my old truck and go talk to people who've asked me to recount parts of my chaotic life for them. I'll speak from home or elsewhere, in France or not, in schools and prisons, in churches and at conferences, in stadiums and in public squares...

My witness is that forgiveness is the most difficult act to come by. It is the most worthy of man. My most beautiful struggle.

L'amour c'est mon poing final…Love is my last word.*

Henceforth, I walk in the way of peace.

* [This is a play on words between the homonyms point and poing; the expression "love is my last word" being rendered "love is my final 'fist' (or 'blow')." *Trans.*]

Chapter 1

Age Three
Abandoned in a Ditch

She didn't kiss me, she didn't say goodbye. Nothing, not a word. This woman moves away from me. She wears white boots... I'm three years old and my mother straps me to a phone pole on this country road that leads to nowhere.

She goes to her car that's parked on the shoulder, moves away, disappears. All I see is fog. I stretch out my arms. I'm alone. Night falls on the forest and its monsters emerge from the shadows.

That's the only clear childhood memory I have of my mother. A back, moving away, and big white boots. Someone leaving... She had me when she was sixteen and abandoned me three years later, the day she went off with the new man in her life. In her existence there was no more room for me.

The police found me the next morning, freezing cold and terrified. They brought me back to my father's house. I don't know how they tracked him down; I couldn't speak.

My father was a bodyguard in an embassy in Paris. He was a slender man, tall as an oak, with a hooked nose and the black hair of his ancestors. This silent athlete couldn't deny his Indian blood.

He was exceptionally strong and his power would be unleashed in one terrifying blow, like lightning, like a bow being released.

My grandmother once told me she'd seen him in a bar being mocked by three brainless greenhorns, saying nothing, his expression unchanged. When one of them tried to provoke him by brushing his sleeve, he was the first of the three to wind up groggy on the floor in less time than it takes to tell the story. Meanwhile, my father was back at the bar ordering another beer as if he'd just brushed off his shoulder or shooed away a fly.

He was the son of a warlord whom I never met, but whose blood flows in my veins. I'm proud of my grandfather. He was an Indian artist who joined the Canadian military as a fighter pilot in the Second World War. He was taken prisoner by the Nazis who mistook him for a Jew because he was circumcised. They sent him to a death camp in Germany. This Iroquois was so honored by their error that he never wanted to disabuse his executioners. He died a few months before the end of the war, after three years of inhuman treatment. My grandmother received only these few words: "I am proud to die with my Jewish brothers."

This courageous woman could never truly believe that the man she loved so passionately, whom she called "the Golden Hand," might be dead. Among the huts of a northern French suburb, in a former munitions depot, she was alone to raise her thirteen children. The two children of one of her daughters were added when their mother was shot for participating in the Resistance. She didn't receive her war-widow's pension until five years after France was liberated, but it came in U.S. dollars… With that she was able to purchase several lots that she gave to each of her children.

My father was also Canadian, but served with the American Marine commandos during the Vietnam War. He saved the life of his lieutenant, who never forgot this gesture: having become a diplomat several years later, he took my father under his protection.

My father had a chink in his armor. My mother's departure cut him off at the knees, like a shot to the heart. He crumbled. He hadn't seen a thing coming.

Having become unstable and unpredictable—he'd started drinking more and more—he turned me over to one of his sisters who lived nearby.

With this tender woman I had my first taste of the happiness that comes from being loved. I learned to stand and walk, to touch the trunks of the trees to which I entrusted my secrets, and to dream in front of medieval tapestries. The blood of my warrior ancestors would boil at the sight of the furious charges and ferocious battles they depicted. This happiness, this sweet anesthesia, was only too short-lived.

A few months later my father came to take me back. I found out that my family had grown: he was living with a woman who looked like an Italian mama, dark, full-figured. She had five children. They had moved into our house as if it were their own.

My father said: "Here's your new mother, give her a kiss. You can call her 'Mama'..."

I could feel the turmoil within me. In spite of my burning desire to find a new mother, I refused to call her "mama." This woman had eyes as dark as the deepest cave. I didn't see in them the slightest glimmer of love. She pinched my arm as she kissed me with a sardonic, hypocritical and vicious smile.

I knew she would never be my mother. She captured my father's heart, but she would never replace the one who bore me. The one who left me one evening along the side of a road, turning her back to me, wearing those tall white boots. I never understood why.

Chapter 2

Age Four
In the Dog House

I reside with my fake family, I eat with them, I sleep with them. I don't live with them. I'm just a stranger. They treat me like an undesirable parasite.

In the evening I expect my father like a Savior. I await his return with an impatience I can't begin to hide. I listen for his footsteps in the stairwell. His key in the lock opens for me the doors of hope. Turning toward this mighty figure, my whole being quietly begs for a glance, a smile. All in vain. He rushes to my fake mother, my fake brothers and my fake sisters. He hugs them, touches them and caresses them as if he wanted to hurt me and exact his revenge, saying: "Here's what you won't have! You remind me too much of your mother, that woman I couldn't hold on to, I couldn't make happy."

I'm the reminder of love lost, of a failed marriage, a symbol of dishonor, his living regret.

My fake mother notices his resentment toward me and triumphantly blurts out: "Your little bastard did it again, today!" He turns toward me, finally, but it's not to take me in his arms. Hope turns to nightmare as his expression changes; the beast growls then pounces. I bite my lips so as not to cry out under the violence of the blows. Slam! Slam! Slam!

As they rain down, my fake mother smiles, savoring the moment. I don't belong in her courtyard, I'm nothing but a lame duckling. She's good to her children, but I'm not part of her brood.

With my father away for several weeks, she chases me out of the house, into the back yard for entire afternoons. In that junk heap surrounded by a large brick wall, like a prison, I find things I recognize. My comrades in exile are rusted bikes, a broken wheelbarrow, a barrel laying on its side and a chain. At the end of that chain is a brown and white pointer: my friend Simla.

In the middle of the courtyard is an enormous basin. The step-mom's kids roll it into the kitchen so they can be indoors in the warmth when it's time to wash up. When they're done grooming, the mother and her eldest haul the tub out back and say: "Here runt, wash up!"

The water is dirty and freezing. Even in winter I have to get in it, shivering. My half-brothers taunt me from the window as they enjoy cookies and colored lollypops. I can see their smiles and the faces they're making through the mist. I stay outside, shivering, until someone comes to get me. I would feel that cold in my body until I was fourteen. The chill reaches the marrow in my bones.

At times I'm so cold I go hide naked in Simla's dog house. My friend the dog howls in protest to remind the humans that they shouldn't treat one of their little ones this way. I love this affectionate pointer. He also gets beaten on a regular basis. It makes us accomplices. I have the feeling he understands me. As soon as I sit in that freezing tub, he starts gently whimpering, to encourage me: "Go for it, Tim, I'm with you." He starts getting on my step-mom's nerves and she comes running out into the yard to beat Simla, and bawl me out while she's at it, calling us dirty bastards. Simla and I are from the same race. This dog is my first friend.

From the time my mother left, my father started binge drinking, more and more. I want to make it clear that this was not because he was Iroquois — it was because like many people whose life drowns them in sorrow and pain, he drowned his own sorrows in alcohol.

Whenever I step into his line of sight, his deadened eyes emerge from their zombie-like stare. Just seeing me lights his fuse. He raises his enormous body, and like a panting lumberjack comes down on me ever more violently. He doesn't need an excuse. I have to hide to avoid causing an explosion.

And yet, every night, I still hope that he'll take me in his arms. I hope against all hope. I can't give up the only thought that keeps me alive.

On a weekend when my fake family is heading off to the country, my father locks me in the cellar. I refuse to go down those steep stairs, so he just pushes me down with a single blow. I tumble down the concrete steps, all the way to the bottom of this dark and humid lair. The closing door shuts out the light. I stay there, groggy on the cold floor, breathing the putrid smells of mold and damp mixed with piss and dog crap. There's a small opening onto the courtyard, right behind Simla's dog house. I get up and slip my hand through the hole. The dog comes and licks my fingers, whimpering. We keep each other company during endless hours of boredom.

On the dark walls of my prison, I hang the imaginary portraits of the three people who showed tenderness and made me happy: my aunt, my maternal grandfather, whom I idolized, and my paternal grandmother. I converse with them in endless monologues, carefully dusting and removing the slightest shadow that might tarnish the brilliance of my inner suns.

I yell at them as well for leaving me with my father. In my darkness I cry out to them: "Come get me, come get me, take me away!"

Sometimes my paternal grandmother comes and takes me out for a day. She's nice and joyful and spoils me, like any grandmother. She buys me clothes, shiny shoes and licorice. But the hours go by and I turn sullen at the thought that this idyllic life will come to an end. She can't understand my somber expression. In the evening she brings me back to the house, my father grabs me by the arm and I cry: "No, no, Grandma, take me with you, take me with you!"

I want so much to stay with her. She leaves without me. I can't tell her that her son beats me. I'm alone with my secret.

Until one day when a family friend comes to have a drink at the house. My father is already drunk. When he tries to give me my daily thrashing, this man gets in his way. My father goes crazy and comes after him with a knife. Bleeding, the friend manages to get out and find his way to a hospital.

The next day, a woman knocks at the door. She asks to see me.

My fake mother refuses. The woman calmly asserts her authority, then finally threatens my step-mom with serious consequences. She gives in and calls me to the door. The woman invites me out for a walk. She's pretty and sweet. Still, I'm afraid. She takes me to a café, offers me a cup of hot chocolate and asks me lots of questions about the family, about my father, whether he's nice and how he takes care of me. I answer without lying; without telling the whole truth. She wouldn't believe me.

Then the nice lady looks at her watch and gets up to take me home. I don't want to go. I hold onto her saying: "I want to stay with you." She explains that she's from Social Services and that she'll make sure no one beats me anymore. I believe her.

As soon as the door is shut, my father yells: "What did you tell her?" He takes a wooden paddle and beats me, and beats me, and beats me. I fall to the floor from the searing pain in my legs. They won't hold me up anymore. He keeps beating and screaming.

"Do you hear me? What did you tell that broad?" Slam! Slam!

"Huh? What did you tell that bitch?"

Slam, Slam! I'm lost in my head. I still believe in that woman. But she never should have left me alone. I tell my father nothing. Slam!

Then he picks me up off the floor by my shirt, carries me like a sack of potatoes, opens the cellar door and sends me flying down the stairs, screaming: "Dirty runt! Zip it or I'll...!"

I don't hear the rest. I fall into a black hole. Flying leap, crash and burn on the landing.

A few seconds later—or a few minutes, I don't know—I come out of it only to hear my step-mom screaming through the haze in my skull: "Get up here, you runt! Come on, get back up here!"

I can't. I can't even move. My fall fractured my jaw and my nose.

My legs are broken. This wretched woman comes down the stairs and starts beating me too. "Come on, move it! Get up there, you runt, get up there!"

Slam, Slam! I crawl, climbing each step like a slug. Slam! Slam! She takes a belt to my back. I can't feel my legs.

My head is spinning. My father is towering over me at the top of the stairs. His blows start raining down on me. One gets me in the eye, another catches the left side of my face, already covered with bruises. The peel of that blow pops my ear. Crack. Darkness. A black hole.

After that I don't remember anything.

It's the day of my fifth birthday.
Instead of a candle from my father, I get lights out!

Chapter 3

Age Five and Six
Silence, Hospital

Three days later I emerge from the darkness of a coma.

I awake to a bright room. Where am I?

I can't move. My body is completely immobilized.

There's a face right near mine. It's smiling. After a few seconds I recognize the social worker. Her gentle gaze is on me. I can't bring myself to hold against her the fact that she left me in the middle of a hurricane. She kept her word.

She says: "You're in the hospital. Don't worry, you won't be afraid anymore."

Those words remain etched in my soul like an enigma. Who can make such a promise: "You won't be afraid anymore"? Fear is like a virus, penetrating your body, your heart, your soul, it digs down deep and penetrates every cell. You don't get to choose whether or not you'll be afraid. It sneaks up on you and grabs you by the throat.

A second time, she says: "You'll never be afraid again."

I only half believe her. Once bitten, twice shy...

I ask her a strange question: "What about my father; is he dead?" "No," she answers. "He's been stripped of his parental rights." For years I would tell anyone who asked me about my father that he'd been stripped of his parental rights without ever knowing what those words meant. I preferred the vagueness of ignorance to a truth that was all too cruel.

and people come by to congratulate me. I get a few "commissions."

Finally, I exist, I'm being recognized. I hug my magic paper that's restoring my legs, flattering me and revealing my hidden talent.

The only obstacle in my rehabilitation is the stairs. I'm afraid of them. I have a terrible fear of steps because I still have no feeling in my right foot. I have to slide my leg forward to keep my foot on the ground. I go down the stairs backwards, gripping the railing and keeping my eyes on the landing so as not to succumb to the fear and panic of falling backward.

In two and a half years in the hospital, I didn't get a single visit, and not a bit of news of my family. I don't know whether my father's alive. I'd rather not know.

Chapter 4

Age Seven
The Orphan Market

The time has come to leave the sterile world of the hospital, its regimented life, its set rituals, where I've woven a protective cocoon for myself. I'm seven and a half. I can walk fairly normally. My right eye is damaged, one ear is swollen, I have a broken nose and a scar across my forehead. I suffer from horrendous headaches that crush my brain like a sharp-edged vise. But I can walk and I can draw.

In order to recover completely, I'm sent to a rehabilitation center on the island of Ré. I get turned out pretty quickly for being overly excitable. The exact same thing happens at Dax. I end up in a nunnery in Arcachon. The Sisters of St. Vincent de Paul are patient and attentive. I remember their white caps and the blue medal that one of them gave me, walks along the pier—the kids my age are buying balloons and candy; meanwhile, I have nothing but holes in my pockets—walks in the sweet smelling shade of the pine trees where I find shelter from the summer heat, and the home of happiness. That's what I named a big white house where I had seen children laughing and playing, running along the terrace between the sea and sky. I promise myself that later, once I'm a man, I'll marry a girl from this place. A girl from the home of happiness...

Now that I've fully recovered, I find myself opening another door onto the world of lost children.

After a long drive and after throwing up everything I had in me, I emerge from my nausea in front of long row of sinister looking buildings, rather poorly suited to relieve my ailing condition. It's the Social Service center of a town in Northern France. With a social worker leading the way, I enter one of the wings of this hospice. We're following hallways filled with elderly people whose clothing smells like pee. A few old folks are crying hysterically. From my well-traveled seven years of age, I watch in awe this hidden world of men and women from another age, with their blank expressions.

A little old lady grabs my arm with a veiny, grayish hand. Her mouth reveals no teeth, just a black hole with chapped lips then, suddenly, her tongue darts out like a pink snake. She stares at me with bulging eyes ready to pop out of their sockets.

In the middle of the hallway is a legless old man with his mouth open, sitting motionless in a wheelchair, like a statue. In a corner on the left, a disheveled man with black hair is banging his head rhythmically against the wall, then he turns around and lets out an odd-sounding laugh through his nose. My stomach starts to turn at seeing the suffering and distress of these waning lives, abandoned and thrown together any old which way.

We're entering a room with beige walls. There's the same stifling smell of must and pee mingled with the stench of ether. There are people playing cards and dominoes. An old lady stops me on my way by. She lays her parchment hand on my arm and offers me some vanilla pudding. She's staring at me with an inconsolable gaze, her head resting on her hollow shoulder, her small black eyes shining like patent leather shoes. I see sadness in her eyes as they rest upon me, and tears begin to well up. With a movement of her hand she bids me farewell. The social worker's calling me; she's upset. I turn one last time toward this old woman of sorrow. She's so beautiful in her silence… Grandma.

Some expressions prove the reality of eternity. Hidden away in our secret chests, these forgotten treasures will awaken again at our moment of doubt. I'll never forget this woman's extraordinary and dignified beauty.

At the end of a long, winding hallway, the social worker indicates a dark red, leather bench next to an enormous staircase: "Have a seat."

Another boy is already sitting there. "Did you pass by the crazies?" he asks, as he puts his finger to his temple and laughs out loud. He's making fun of them, and I'm offended.

The social worker returns. My neighbor gives me a worried look. He squints and mouths something in a whisper. Fear grips me. What's he saying? The door opens. The woman is speaking softly to another one who nods in my direction with a stern look on her face. The second woman assigns me a number made up of my birth date and of the county where I was born. I get undressed. I get vaccinated. Then they shave my head, cover me with some potent smelling ointment and wrap my head with bandages. I think I look pretty good as an oil Sheik. "It's to kill the lice," she explains.

She sends me into a large room. About thirty other kids are there, with their heads shaved, standing in a line. We're all dressed the same: plaid Bermuda shorts, T-shirt and boots. We're all blankly staring at each other. I ask permission to go see my teary-eyed old woman. I'm not allowed to. "Listen here! Don't you go anywhere!"

My mummy costume is taken from me and I'm told to go join the others at the end of the line, side by side, along the large staircase, near the main door. It's Thursday, no school.

Suddenly the door opens. About forty men and women enter the room. Some of them are all dressed up, like on a Sunday, others are dressed in rags. They wend their way through our group, looking at us as if we were rare artifacts or displays from the wax museum. They watch, scrutinizing every detail from head to toe. Then there are the expressive ones —"Oh, look how cute this one is! I really like him!"—and the ones who don't show any of their emotions, studying us in silence, occasionally emitting a grunt of satisfaction before one of us. There are those who ask questions, and those who furrow their brow, two fingers pressed against their cheek, a pensive look on their face, as if they were trying to imagine how this boy might turn out in a few years. Some pass by again and again, like the bettors at a horse race, writing down the number each of us is wearing on his chest.

These people have come to choose a child.

At noon they all clear the area once they're done shopping for abandoned children. Only two boys are left in this large, spartan room, a boy named Christian and me. The others were all adopted. For Christian, this is his second time he's gotten his hopes up. No luck. He's only got one chance left. He explains the rules of the game to me:

"If you're not chosen by the third time, you go off to a correctional home. You've got three tries in all..."

After a moment of silence, he adds: "Do you know why no one took us?"

"Well, no... I have no idea."

"It's because we're not good looking. People like good looking children."

It's true, Christian's really not very good looking. And I must be as ugly as he is since I wasn't among the chosen either.

The evening comes and I can't sleep. I lay awake dreaming of a pretty lady and a nice, well-dressed man coming up to me and taking me out of the lineup: "Come with us." They take me by the hand and I see myself, between the two of them, crossing the large threshold of this building in a halo of light.

It's a dream that keeps me from sleeping. I often roll it over in my mind, awaiting D-day, the day of my deliverance.

The following Thursday, there's the same ceremony with ten new boys. I get brought up in a few huddles and whispered conversations. I don't get chosen. The pretty lady and the nice, well-dressed man didn't come. Christian and I are left on the spot again, like the damaged produce that the shopkeepers can't get rid of and leave out after the market closes. We're children that have been beaten and gone bad.

A gloomy afternoon. That evening we're alone, back in our dismal dormitory. We're so sad inside. Christian blew his last chance. He'll be going off to a correctional home. I don't want him to leave me. He's my comrade in abandonment.

The other boys are sleeping in a big bed, with clean sheets, in a beautiful house, with a father and a mother taking care of them. Good for them. We didn't win the love lottery. Too bad for us.

As the dorm lights go out, I'm suddenly afraid. I start crying. My father's coming back to beat me. Why is this obsessive fear gripping me so much more strongly than usual? I scream. Someone throws cold water on me. I tear the sheets with my teeth.

"Go ahead and cry. That'll be one less time you need to go to the bathroom!" says the night monitor.

On that night, I start closing the gates to my heart and drying up the flow of tears. Unless I want to die or go crazy, I have to harden my heart.

The next morning I get introduced to a woman psychologist. She doesn't even look me over. She glances at my file and concludes that I'm ill. "What with?" I ask. Long silence. I stare at her. I'm actually feeling pretty healthy. She makes extensive notes on a sheet of paper.

"Next!" she says, without even looking at me.

Someone grabs me by the arm and I'm off to somewhere by car. I have no idea where we're going. Suddenly I get this crazy thought in my head. A glimmer of happiness. I ask the woman who's driving: "Are you taking me to my mother?"

She says yes.

The nightmare's over.

Chapter 5

Age Eight
The Lunatic Prison

She said yes.

The bitch lied to me, and I believed her for a minute.

Our trip's over and so is the dream. My mother's not the one waiting at the end of this long, tree-lined drive, it's a castle for crazy people. A residential clinic.

The elation that came over me for a few minutes is suddenly gone, like a punctured balloon. It gives way to disgust and anger. I don't trust anyone anymore. Why did she say yes? To avoid touchy questions? To have some peace and quiet during the three hour ride?

Last Thursday I lost the love lottery, today I won a game of "despair Bingo."

Life in the castle gets off to a bad start. I'm greeted by a sinister looking man in a blue outfit. We go inside. I hear shrieks and muffled sniggering. It's a zoo where men live in cages. It's not open to the public.

On this day I find myself violently struck by a strange, silent suffering. A world is crumbling within me. I watch, I listen, I wait. Every second, every minute, every hour, every day that goes by is one I can't begin to understand. The sum of my fears is growing like an abyss I'm helpless to fill. I'm getting sucked in. I'm needle shy. The medication is slowly eroding my awareness.

I'm regressing, turning into a zombie. Inside my head I have the feeling I'm turning in circles. Tiny circles. I'm fighting to keep my balance, to keep from passing out. I don't want any of their crap. I try to run. The orderlies grab me and hold me down to stick me with needles.

For nine months, I keep turning in circles. My life is suffering, my soul is suffering. Some scream, others groan. Shrieks, frantic silence. Empty stares, frozen postures, stiffened limbs, mechanical steps, slowed movements, husky voices, screeching... All the unbearable details that are being etched within me every day. All the unbearable secrets of these men and women, whom their families have had committed in order to acquire their inheritance or to revoke their custody of a child. Some were turned in by a neighbor, a spouse or a son, either out of revenge or for personal gain. Sometimes for no reason at all. That's what these people tell me. Can I believe them? It's too late. The general suspicion of insanity is lurking and annihilates any trust. The connection is broken, the number you're trying to reach has been disconnected. It's every man for himself in his straight jacket. It's a trip to hell. The day to day flows by me without ever really touching me, but I never manage to dissociate from myself enough to keep from suffering. It's not total anesthesia. Step by step, I struggle against the fog that's winning out, trying to get inside me. At times my eyes well up and I get a knot in my throat. Every second that goes by is interminable, horrendously long and laden with threats.

I'm living in fear of fear. It hides during the day and pounces at night. Once I lie down, these horrific images return to nail me violently to my bed. I can hide, close my eyes, scream "No, no!" under my breath and reject them with all my strength, but it's no use. My past is stalking me, clawing away. My father, my fake mother, thc cellar stairs, the lineup of abandoned kids, Christian's "we're not good looking," "You're right, we're not good looking," the liar that said yes and the lunatic asylum at the end of the row of trees, instead of my mother...

Every night, these monsters return, leap at my throat and wake me up. I keep colliding with these painful memories.

I'm not crazy. That certainty within me is what spares me from dementia. My only folly is having been born into a human world. My only dream is of a kiss, a hug. My only hope is for a hand to put mine in and a tender, smiling gaze. In my head I'm moving in slow motion and I hear a soft, quiet voice within me, a whisper of love. I want so much to believe: mama's going to come get me.

My delusion is such that I convince myself that my father is also going to change. He'll stop drinking. He'll be nice and I'll be able to call him papa. The look in his eyes when he turns toward me won't be like a storm anymore, but like spring. I need so much to believe that. Miracles don't just happen to other people. My delusion is ready to erase the wounds of this life and dares to dream the impossible.

I'm not crazy in my head, doctor, just in my hope.

This same hope is kept alive by boys and girls who've been abandoned like me, and committed like me: they believe in miracles. They say: "My parents will come get me." And it's true, they're right. One day, one beautiful day, a man and a woman come to pick them up. It's such a beautiful thing to see these brothers and sisters returning to a family.

One late morning, after nine months of being locked up, I'm taken to see the new psychiatrist. He's a big man, well-groomed well-dressed. He looks at me kindly and invites me to have a seat at a small table. He gives me some puzzles and asks me to put them together. No problem. He asks me some odd questions, riddles. I answer. It's a breeze. As he's going about his interrogation, I start drawing. I offer him my sketch. He's surprised and starts looking at me attentively. I explain to him that drawing is my secret language. When I'm drawing I enter into a world of beauty, where everything is free. I leave indifference and contempt behind for the joy of pleasing others.

The psychiatrist looks at my drawing and pats me on the head saying: "You're sly and you're talented. Keep it up, my boy, keep drawing."

He gives me a broad smile and leans on a ringer. A man enters. The doctor asks him: "What's this boy doing here? He's perfectly well!"

As the other one feigns ignorance, the doctor addresses me: "Farewell young man!"

Then, gently pinching my cheek, he says: "You're not sick, you're fine. You've got to keep drawing."

I don't want to leave him.

Nine months ago, a doctor that looked me over for a few seconds declared that I was crazy, deranged, abnormal. Nine months later, another doctor took a look at me, examined me and declared that I was fine. The first filled out her report without looking up. The second welcomed me and asked me questions, gently and attentively. He tried to look beyond my appearance. This man freed me not only from the asylum but also, in a way, from another, inner prison.

I can't quite fathom what just happened. I head back to the dormitory to pick up a few things. An orderly asks me to follow him. I get into his ambulance and he sets off, tires screeching, sirens blaring, as if I were seriously injured.

We stop off at Social Services. A lady says to me: "Put your finger on this pad, push hard, then put it over here."

I leave my mark in a notebook. Now I'm listed. I'm not just a number, I'm also a finger... there's human progress after all. You can change a number, but not a finger print. It's one of a kind. That doesn't change the fact that for years I was called not by my name but by my number.

Chapter 6

Age Nine
In the Clutches of the Guardian

Four of us from Social Services get placed in foster care with a farmer. She took us in for the money. This woman is mean, greedy and ugly. A dragon with matted hair put up in a greasy bun. A wicked fairy whose boots I have to shine every morning. I hate her with my whole heart, from the depths of my soul. Especially since I had hoped so much for her love.

The witch makes me feed the animals in the evening and polish the furniture in the morning. All the chores keep me from getting my homework done, so the bad grades start piling up at school, and those get me slapped and bawled out... It's a vicious cycle. Bawled out at school, bawled out at home.

Her favorite form of torture is to make me walk bare-legged in a pit of nettles, in a ditch that runs along a nearby field, making me repeat idiotic resolutions about milking the cows and speaking formally to people my age after I've just used a familiar tone with one of my peers who's actually three months younger than I am... What I find most revolting is that this woman calls herself a Christian. That bigot won't let me eat meat or eggs because I'm not baptized, she says. For the same reason, the Swiss guy, this ecclesiastical bodyguard who parades around in a Napoleonic carnival outfit during the services and keeps his eye on me during Sunday Mass, makes me put my head down so I don't look at the host during the consecration. "You're not worthy," he told me one day. So I put my head down and imagine myself giving him a swift kick in the nuts. At least the choirboys' bells would have a good reason to jingle...

My guardian-torturer forces me to go to church. Not to discover God but to wax the pews and floors. She's obsessed with keeping everything spotless and shiny; she's like a wax maniac.

I'm so hungry that, on a morning when I'm supposed to be cleaning the floors, I take advantage of being alone in this dank, country temple to open up the tabernacle. I uncork one of the golden flasks, grab the little white wafers and start eating. I empty the cup and stuff myself with hosts.

I learned later, from persons in charge, that those were consecrated. That in what appears to be round and pale pieces of bread, in each of those light morsels are contained the whole humanity and the whole divinity of Jesus Christ, the God-man who dwelt among men. In the theft of a starving child, which I committed, I've just had my first communion. For the time being, I don't know a thing about the mysteries, about the sin of gluttony, or about what some would call blasphemy.

I'm filling up on Christ without even knowing it. This innocent sacrilege was no doubt foreshadowing another hunger, the hunger for God who alone can heal the wounds of love and satisfy the heart of man.

I empty the sacred vessels of their contents, then the reserve from the sacristy. I have an orgy of hosts.

At noon, as I get back to the farm, my shipmates are already sitting down to lunch. My hands are so cold that I can't hold my fork. The bitch pulls my plate away saying: "Too bad, if you don't want to eat. You'll see it again tonight..."

Here I go spending another afternoon on empty. I'm sick of it. God's bread doesn't carry much weight in my empty stomach.

Is it today that the priest is coming over for dinner? He starts lecturing me: "Remember, my boy, you're not baptized... If you die, we won't be able to bury you in the human cemetery, we'll have to bury you with the animals!"

Well, that takes care of that, old priest. I'd rather be buried among the beasts than among Christians. At least the animals are nice.

I refuse to join the Church of this Catholic-certified guardian of mine that offers me nothing but hell instead of Heaven.

One day the Social Services lady drops by for a surprise visit. The guardian says I'm not there—I can hear that snake through floor boards—even though I'm just one flight up, polishing the floor. I head downstairs; it's my one opportunity. I'm hoping the woman will detect her lie and realize that something's not right in this wretched house. But the hypocrite catches me at the bottom of the stairs: "Oh, you were here, Philip dear? I didn't know. Isn't it true that you're happy here?"

Every morning I wax things for her, I put my heart into it, I put my best effort into this repetitive gesture hoping for nothing more than a look of gratitude or a word from her: "That's lovely!" If once, only once, she had said: "Bravo, that's beautiful," I think that, in spite of her cruelty, I might have been able to eke out: "Yes, I'm happy here." But all she ever had for me was contempt. "What do you say, Philip, you're happy here, right?" This wicked bigot is pinching my shoulder and twisting my skin. You'd think the Social Services people had shit in their eyes! I answer nothing and head back up the stairs four at a time. Tears of hatred run silently down my cheeks.

The guardian's showing the inspector around the upstairs. "...and here are the two rooms; each boy has his own bed." I want to scream: "Don't listen to her, the bitch is lying! We don't sleep here. Those beds are there only so she can get the money from Social Services. We sleep on rotten mattresses out in the barn!"

I want to let all that out and all kinds of other things as well, but no one would believe me and I'm so weary.

A month ago I tried committing suicide by throwing myself from a huge pile of tree trunks in a nearby forest. A lumberjack died that way, by accident. His death is what gave me the idea.

So I launched myself from the top of this wooden pyramid, hoping to find the great sleep at the bottom, but all I got was bruises, scratches and aches and pains.

On August 9th, on my birthday, I decide to try again, and to do it right this time. I hurt too much. I want it to stop. Horrendous migraines have been crushing my skull—maybe it's the hunger? And all those blows I took… I'm tired of being on the receiving end, tired of suffering.

On the night of my birthday, I get up and make my way to the outhouse at the far end of the courtyard. I tie a rope to a beam, climb up on the throne and throw myself off with no hesitation.

The knot tightens around my neck, it starts strangling me, then I hear a loud craaack. The worm-eaten woodwork caves in, tiles start falling on top of me. I'm sitting in shit and start crying.

I really can't do anything right. Even death doesn't want me! Tonight, I'm turning nine and I'm literally in deep shit…

A few days later, out of spite, the guardian pushes me against the edge of a metal bed while I'm sweeping her room. The pain is excruciating and my arm is dangling, limp. She makes me wash the dishes and keep repeating: "It doesn't hurt, it doesn't hurt…"

It hurts more and more.

The next day, she has to take me to the hospital. As they examine my broken arm with its yellow and black hues, the doctors start asking me questions. I tell them what happened. They start pushing to get more out of me and I tell them about the guardian's abuse.

The medical personnel sound the alarm at Social Services. There's an immediate inquiry. Other boys from the village tell them that I often complain about being hungry and that I get stomach cramps and headaches.

I get pulled from the farm just before my third attempt at quitting this life and getting myself out of hell.

A mildly plump woman with a bit of a mustache and a pony tail comes to pick me up, and we're off. We drive along in silence for about an hour, out in the country. After about sixty kilometers we pull into a muddy courtyard. Another farm, I clench my fists. We pull up next to a big pile of manure. The social worker is afraid of slipping, so she tiptoes along, disgusted by the lingering smells. It doesn't bother me anymore, not since the hospital, the asylum and the bigot's farm.

We're greeted by a woman with a scarf around her head. The social worker turns to me and says: "This is where you're going to live now. Be good."

The two women begin talking quietly. I start listening to the sounds around the farm, the clucking, the quacking... The social worker leaves. The woman takes me inside, into a dark, inviting kitchen with wonderful smells: "Are you hungry, or thirsty? Do you want anything?"

I don't answer, I stay on the defensive. Is this another witch?

"Cat got your tongue?"

I stay silent. Suddenly a dark-skinned little man enters the kitchen, a beret on his head and a cigarette butt at one corner of his mouth. He looks nice. He smiles at me: "So there you are!"

As if he'd been expecting me for a while. This is the husband of the woman with the scarf.

The woman serves me a bowl of soup, adding: "You can say 'thank you, mama.'"

There's silence within me. There's something in the way.

Rejection. How can I say "mama" to a woman who's not my mother? You only get one, and that's for life. I don't touch the soup. The little man empties his bowl rather loudly. After that he shows me the house and my room, upstairs: "This is your home."

I go back down to the kitchen, still silent. He just says: "Are you coming, son?"

I follow him outside. We get up on his orange tractor. He invites me to sit to his left, on a metal seat. He's looking at me, his eyes are bright, he seems happy...

"How are you, li'l tyke? Let's go..."

"Li'l tyke," as I found out later, means "little one." But right away I felt that there was love in that word.

As we head through the village on the tractor, the farmer starts waving to everyone, like a president going down the Champs-Élysées on Bastille Day. I'm feeling proud and a little bit insecure at the same time, riding along on this contraption that keeps bouncing on its oversized tires at every bump in the road. I just hold on tight. First we're on our way to see Granny Charlotte, then off to Uncle George's, his wife's brother. They're all light-hearted and friendly. My adopted father, whose name is Gabe, introduces me saying: "Here's the li'l tyke we went to get in town... Here's our li'l tyke..."

He gets thirsty a lot, so we stop off to see this person and that person, have some coffee here, some coffee there, always in a nice friendly atmosphere. Everyone seems to get along in this village. Once we get back to the farm, it's time to pay a visit to the cows, then the pigs—their grunting makes me nervous—the rabbits, the chickens, the Barbary Coast ducks, recognizable by their charred crests, the guinea hens and the turkeys.

"Hey, li'l tyke, come see the baby calf," my new papa says to me. He starts mixing up a bucket of powdered milk and water. After dipping his fingers in the mixture, he slips them into the mouth of this little black and white calf that's lying in the hay.

"Look here, li'l tyke: you put your hand in his mouth, it tickles him and he starts sucking." I try it out and the calf starts sucking on my fingers. His large, questing eyes are so moving.

After milking the cows, we head back to the house. It's dark out. I just turned nine and I've got a wicked fear of the dark. The church bells start clanging. I'm scared. "Yeah, someone died," says my new papa. The night is like a tunnel echoing with those eerie bells. The return trip isn't a happy one. Mister Gabe senses my fear and pats me on the leg: "Don't worry—I'm here, li'l tyke." I find his gesture and his words are reassuring.

Suddenly, the house emerges from the shadows with its lit windows.

"Come wash your hands, li'l tyke."

My foster father, as they say at Social Services, passes me the soap. His cigarette butt is managing acrobatic feats on his lower lip. He takes off his beret and, to my great surprise, uncovers a big white bald spot on top of his head.

At the dinner table I settle in next to him, proudly. He starts perusing the paper with an occasional glance in my direction. I feel like I exist for him. My new mother also looks at me with bright, wrinkled, caring eyes. She's missing a few teeth. She's kind of intimidating with the scarf on her head, her red cheeks and gnarled hands. She serves up the soup in large hollowed out plates. On the table is a fourth setting that's still empty, with no one to claim it. I start wondering why, when a young girl walks in. She's medium height, shoulder-length brown hair, with a round face and kind eyes. It's their daughter, Françoise. She looks me right in the eye and gives me a self-assured greeting. The meal is delicious. I relish the wonderful smells of this kitchen.

Françoise, my new sister, is in a home-making school. Her room is right next to mine. After dinner, I go exploring on the sly. There, on her table, under a cloth, I discover an enormous cake. It looks so good I can't resist having a piece. I take a bite, she catches me with my mouth full and scolds me… rather nicely considering I'd just devoured the cake she had so carefully prepared for a contest at school! I'm the only one who knows that she deserves the best grade!

Her father laughs, her mother worries, wondering whether it'll make me sick. My foster father reassures her: "Our li'l tyke is strong as a Turk, he could swallow an anvil!"

I have no idea what a Turk is, but I like him calling me "our li'l tyke."

To think that a few days ago I wanted to die…

I fall asleep with a full stomach, licking my lips, without any sad dreams, thinking of my friend the little black and white calf, and especially of this man who, for the first time in my life, calls me "my little one." Tomorrow, I'll call him papa.

Chapter 7

Age Ten
Happiness Up in Smoke

The day after my arrival on Papa Gabe's farm, I head off to school on foot, with a brand new book bag over my shoulder.

I'm the biggest and broadest kid in the class, a good head taller than everyone else. Of course, mine is shaved and banged up and pretty noticeable. Because of my size, the teacher puts me in elementary school. I'm nine years old, but I've only been to school fifteen days in my whole life. All I can read is a clock. I'm a well of ignorance and I've just skipped the first two classes.

One morning, this dull, dry woman asks me to go to the board and write down a dictation. Since I can't write I start drawing the story of this text that she's reading and articulating so slowly: A horse, a carriage and a man who looks like Papa Gabe. The whole class starts laughing at my fresco. The teacher thinks I'm mocking her, comes toward me in a rage and starts pulling my right ear. Ouch! That ear's my imperiled masterpiece. I wince at the pain. She starts screaming at me, but I've already learned how to shut all that out. With my father I perfected a technique for self-preservation: I go into a ball, deep inside myself, like a porcupine, and I wait for the storm to pass. This passive resistance only kindles her wrath. She grabs me, screaming: "Take off your coat and put it on backwards, you dolt!"

Then she puts a funny looking hat on me, with two points, like ears. It strikes me as kind of funny. She hands me a slate and orders me to write: "I'm a dolt." Since I can't write she thinks I've gone on strike. So she writes it herself, trembling with rage, and hangs it on my back before sending me out to do laps around the playground during recess. The other kids start sniggering, pointing fingers and making fun of me... Suddenly, I understand that this isn't a game and that its sole purpose is humiliation.

From that day on, school seemed like nothing more than one long, asinine process. I hate this teacher who makes me do things I don't know how to do, and punishes me for things I'm incapable of doing. She doesn't try to explain anything, or share her knowledge, or make you want to learn. She's too proud ever to admit when she's wrong.

So one night, to get her back, I play my kind of trick on her. I make a skull out of a sugar beet. It's easy. All you have to do is stick some corn silk in the top, for the hair, a couple pieces of coal for the eyes and a turkey bone for the mouth. Then you attach the whole thing to the end of a stick. A buddy of mine and I wait for nightfall. We make our way over to the teacher's house. I knock on the window. She comes up and sees our death mask dangling in front of her, sniggering. She gets scared out of her wits and passes out. I don't feel the slightest regret.

Finally, summer vacation comes around. We go racing through the fields, laughing in the sunshine. I wake up to a crowing rooster, have a nice creamy cup of hot chocolate and head out on the tractor with Papa Gabe to milk the cows in the field. We give each other a knowing look as we breathe deeply the aromas of a countryside just awaking under the morning dew.

Milking a cow is easy, they say, you just have to squeeze the udder. Yeah, right! Marguerite is especially temperamental. One morning, with the slightest nudge of her rump, she knocks my stool over and I go sprawling in a mix of manure and spilt milk. Papa Gabe busts out laughing.

"Hey, li'l tyke, you're going about it all wrong!"

He rolls himself another cigarette and sets it in the corner of his mouth where it'll hang for the next few hours. Then he takes his stool and patiently starts initiating me into the art of milking a cow.

"Look here, like this... without forcing anything, steadily, especially with Rita, because her udder hurts. Rita's beautiful and always gives birth to magnificent calves. Right, Rita?"

He starts petting the beast. The cow is staring at me and moves me with her sad, gentle eyes.

Papa Gabe treats his cows with the tender affection of a father. We bring the milk bottles back to the farm before going off to feed the two hundred boars. The dung heap is steaming, the pigeons are cooing, all's well on this earth where the seeds are beginning to grow. My wounded love is slowly beginning to heal.

One day this beet farmer, a Polish woman, offers me a tiny black puppy. I don't dare say anything to Papa Gabe, so I hide this lovable little pup in the pig pen. I entrust him to a sow that starts taking care of him like one of her own. Then one morning, at breakfast, Papa Gabe says, very solemnly: "Colette, one of the sows had a baby black as coal. We're going to have to put it down."

I get all flustered and my throat tightens. With chocolate milk all around my mouth, I stammer: "No, no, don't kill it... it's not a weird looking pig... ummm... it's a goat!"

They all break out laughing. I'm just confused. Apparently, they'd been following my little saga for a few days.

"Don't worry about it, li'l tyke, we're not going to touch your little pup! Why didn't you tell us? You know, one animal more or less..."

I wanted to hug them!

For years my experience taught me that pain went hand in hand with ugliness. Here, on the farm, I discovered happiness and her kin, beauty. Everything here is true and good, the animals as well as the people. Papa Gabe's no Adonis, he's no model from some magazine, but he's beautiful in his heart, a heart that he opens up for me.

I'm happy, and I'm becoming more and more attached to this new papa. We go together to greet the Poles and the Yugoslavs that come to work the beet fields. Then we go visit the blacksmith who shoes Uncle George's horses. He also builds wagons and fixes tipcarts. Fascinated, I admire this athlete with his massive arms, clad in his leather apron. Camped out in his dark, cave-like lair, he beats the red hot metal in rhythm, breathing out with every stroke, his forehead covered with sweat. This man with his artistic gestures strikes me as all-powerful; he trains the animals, he gains mastery over steel and tames fire. In his tongs, every piece takes on its shape under the roar of the blows. Then it's dipped, immersed in a vat, and in the midst of a cloud of steam, it becomes unique.

The game warden beats his drum on the church square, in front of the monument to the dead. In a theatrical voice he announces a water shortage or a blackout. Or perhaps the coming of the rabbit skin vendor, a road closed for repair, the feast of the harvest, for which all the tractor wagons become flower-laden chariots. Then he goes and has a drink at the local café.

The height of the year is the harvest. All the wagons are filled with wheat and led in procession up to the co-op market. Sitting on top of this treasure I think of myself as a prince. I feel drunk from the sweet smell of warm wheat. A few moments later, I'm amazed at the golden rain pouring into the silo.

We start loading up the hay with pitchforks. The men are laughing as they pile the bales on the wagon. Dripping wet, they toss them up with a thrust of their hips and the grunts of a weightlifter. The enormous load slowly makes its way to the hangars. My new father isn't the least of these workers. I admire him, he's wonderful.

This summer he's teaching me how to drive the tractor. I'm so happy and proud that I make a mistake. Accidentally dropping it into reverse, I back right into Grandma Charlotte's cellar door. The door explodes on impact. There's nothing left but kindling... We came close to a bad accident: the tractor's got one wheel suspended in mid air. Papa Gabe doesn't hold it against me: "That way, next time, you'll know how to put it in reverse!" He uses my mistakes to help me learn. Not like the teacher...

I'm starting to get a taste of the happiness of being loved, thinking maybe it'll last.

One August morning, Paulo, a nephew of Papa Gabe and Colette's, gets the idea to build a straw hut in the barn. He's two years older than I am. We get along well. We had found candles in a bunker that served as a backdrop for many of our games. Paulo lights the candles, they're pretty. The straw catches right away. We hadn't thought about it. We try to put it out. It's too late. I move quickly to get the cows out, they're mooing and frightened. The fire grows more intense, roaring like that forge. In just a few minutes, the barn becomes a giant torch. Paulo runs away. I'm left standing alone in front of this inferno, smoke swirling, flames dancing. I'm afraid. I start running, feeling tremendous sadness, sensing that my happiness is burning along with that barn.

All day long I wander aimlessly along empty paths and through fields, my heart shattered, my face covered with tears of anger and grief.

By the end of the afternoon, I get snagged by the police. They bring me back to the farm. I get bawled out, nothing more. Papa Gabe's not looking well, he seems awkward and avoids looking at me. Colette's face has gone stern, she says nothing. Finally she blurts out: "Someone's coming to get you!"

Those words spell my doom. She'll never forgive me, I know it. In vain I try explaining what happened, but my lot's been cast, the judgment is final. I realize that Paulo's left me holding the bag. The word of a child from Social Services doesn't carry much weight in the balance. I'm the number one suspect and deprived of any recourse.

A kid who comes from nowhere and belongs to no one is always wrong, especially when things start going badly.

I'm going to have to leave the farm and my Papa Gabe.

I can't bear the thought.

Chapter 8

Age Eleven
The Correctional Home,
In with the "Hard Cases"

The very night of the fire, a social worker comes to pick me up. There are no goodbyes. I don't want to leave Papa Gabe, and he doesn't want to leave me either. He's grown attached to me, I know he has. We adopted each other. We can't live without each other anymore. He really sees me as his child, and this separation is tearing his heart to pieces. Colette wears the pants, though, and must have imposed this cruel decision. The shame of having to accept this unjust verdict only adds to his pain.

He doesn't kiss me goodbye so as not to cry. He stays in a corner of the kitchen, looking distraught, his cigarette butt motionless, his eyes on the ground, like a dog that's been beaten. Colette opened her home to me, but not her heart. She didn't kiss me goodbye either. For her, I'm just a boarder. My dream of love comes crashing down like the walls of that barn where there's nothing but charred remains, twisted, blackened metal and ashes that the firemen are still dousing as I climb into the car.

I don't turn around.

This long trip is a descent into hell. I'm guessing, from the stern, stubborn look on the social worker's face, that I'm in for some shock-treatment. My carelessness is being taken for malevolence and it's all so unfair. We both remain silent during the entire trip. I don't want to show this outsider any of my tears, my fear or my rage. As we enter the courtyard of the correctional home, in D., near La Rochelle, I get a brutal awakening.

The director launches into his usual welcome speech: "You'd better keep it on the straight and narrow! We've got our eye on you. Any wild kids around here, we tame 'em, we break 'em and we make 'em toe the line."

They shave my head, dress me in their blue, cotton prison uniform and take me to the refectory. One of the instructors barks: "Go sit with the others!"

I'm released into this arena of wild beasts.

The seventy some boys from that section are staring me down like a fly whose wings they're about to tear out. And this hostile group begins its torture.

As soon as I find a place to sit down, they chase me away: "Take off! Get lost!" They swipe the meat off my plate, then my dessert, all with their hypocritical smiles. I'm being terrorized by these jackals and I don't dare say a thing. The gang leader, the one who keeps swiping my food, catches me in the hallway with his goons. He corners me and starts choking me. "Are you the one who messed with my brother?" No, no, I don't even know who his brother is. He starts threatening and beating me. Every day it's the same thing, a constant fear in the pit of my stomach. I can't seem to make any friends. They've all joined against me, either out of fear or malice.

Neither the instructors nor the kids I'm in with seem to care for this busted up mug of a beaten child that I'm wearing. No one finds me likeable. Anger is rising in me, but fear is still winning out.

One night it all starts overflowing. The fear, the loneliness, the sadness, the despair. I start sobbing, stuffing my sadness into the sheets on my bed. The next day, one of the instructors, who thinks he's Charles Bronson, says to me: "Hey, you blubberer, go ahead and cry in front of everyone!"

All the other kids chime in, mocking: "Cry baby, cry baby…"

I'm so poor I have no right to cry. Expressing my pain is a luxury I don't get to indulge in. My tears have no right to exist, nor to be seen. So I lie in my suffering, I bluff. I close off my heart and stem the flow of my tears. I fight to keep from crying. My nose is stinging, I have a lump in my throat and my chest is tight. But it works.

I turn my tears into anger, into bundles of rage. All the hate I've stored up against undeserved maliciousness and sheer stupidity becomes a fireball spinning within me, looking for a way out. I'm possessed, consumed by a will to crush this rabble that has both scared and disgusted me.

For three months I've put up with threats, accusations, humiliation, punishments, mockery, without a word, without a tear.

One day, at lunch, without any warning, I turn into what I was accused of being: a wild child. The bundle of hatred starts coming out. As usual, the little gang leader stretches out his hand to swipe the meat on my plate with his dirty fingers. I stare him right in the eyes, grab my fork and bury it in his hand. The frightened child I was has turned into a beast. He screams and I just keep staring at him without flinching, without letting go of the fork. All the rage that was stored up over the space of a hundred days is let loose. Three instructors pounce on me. I don't want to let go of this bastard. I'm reveling in his pain. His pierced hand is stuck to my plate like a butterfly on display.

They start hitting me and pulling my clothes and finally get me to let go. I let myself fall backwards. I hop up on the dessert cart, grab a ladle and start hitting the kid who beat me up the night I got here. Revenge is a dish best served cold, sometimes with a fork and a ladle. The instructors tackle me and start thrashing me on the floor, but I can't feel the blows anymore. I've been immune to them since "my most tender childhood"—that expression always made me laugh.

By the time I get back up, I'm in pretty bad shape and my nose is bleeding. I look around at the others, staring them down. I'm free. I'm out from under their tyranny. Free from fear. Up yours!

My promotion is instantaneous. I get transferred to D block.

Section D is for the tough cases. That night I get waxed by my fellow inmates who sneak up on me in my sleep. My revenge is immediate. I grab a couple of toilet plungers, fill them with crap and try to suffocate my assailant with excrement. The instructors come running. Another thrashing.

The dam within me has been shattered. I get a crash course in destruction. I turn fearsome. Now I can feel the violence rising, the way a cook knows that the water in her pressure cooker's about to boil a few seconds before it starts whistling. Thanks to a sixth sense, I start recognizing this tension wherever it manifests itself: out on the football field, in the dormitory stairwell, or in the showers, but I have no fear of its impalpable, rising power, nor of its eruption. I've paid the price, it doesn't scare me anymore.

The next day I get put in isolation, I get thrashed, I get lectured. Another transfer. I wind up on C block. These are the hardened cases, the intractable types. Surprise! I had feared the worst, but instead I get a warm welcome. A nineteen-year-old boy adopts me and calls me "little brother." The instructors are calm, self-assured and they don't play favorites.

At twelve years of age, I'm the youngest of a group of twenty or so boys made up mostly of eighteen- to twenty-year-olds. They're no choirboys. Most of them have run away several times and done some stealing. They tell stories about "the world" and "life," very simply. I stand in awe of these mates, with their numbers and shaved heads, standing before the gates of freedom. What I don't yet realize is that once they turn twenty-one, most of them will be leaving our little prison, but only on their way to a bigger one. The luckier ones will join the Foreign Legion, commandos or disciplinary battalions. To me they're beautiful and genuine. In spite of their strength and their violent nature, they haven't accused me, threatened me, hazed me or persecuted me in any way. These abandoned older brothers have adopted and protected me. I'm fascinated by the stories of their adventures. I can see their wounds, collect their memories and welcome their experience with respect. I feel reverence for this humanity they keep hidden away beneath their tough exteriors. I discover as well that, at twelve years of age, I've already lived what an average twenty-year-old will probably never encounter.

I'm a bit like a brand new car that someone ran wide open on rugged dirt roads. My engine's been overworked and something in me is broken.

The hardest thing about being a wounded child is having to seem bigger, tougher and more mature than you really are. Meanwhile, you're only old enough to be a child. It's having every day to drape the cloak of violence over your frail shoulders when all you want is to wear the mantle of tenderness.

One day the police bring a boy back to the correctional home, an adolescent from C block who had run away for several weeks. He's a tough one—one of the toughest, according to the older brothers who recount his exploits with a hint of fear.

The director calls us all out onto the football field. We line up, as usual. Right in front of us, the instructors start beating the boy, hitting him again and again. That's the custom around here. He slumps to the ground and they keep hitting him, kicking him. Public thrashing, to serve as an example.

"This is how I treat runaways. You can dispose of him!" says the director with this body lying still before him. He turns and walks off.

The ceremony's over, no one dares move. I know I have to go to him. I start moving forward when an older brother catches me: "No, don't go, he can be really mean!"

I don't listen to him. I keep walking toward this prostrate body, lying still on the ground. Standing in front of him, I declare: "One day I'm going to do just what you did."

The boy moves, raises his head, directs an intense stare at me and blinks. His blue eyes reflect the sky. They're bright and pure, not the look of a runaway or a coward. His nose bloodied, he manages to say: "Don't screw around, little brother, they always win!"

Today, in the depths of my heart, this boy has become my hero. This adolescent is like me, with no roots, no identity, just a few years more. I want to surpass my role-model. Looking at his broken nose, pissing blood, I decide to play it smarter than he did and be stronger than these instructors who broke him. I'll wear them down, they'll crack. No matter what the cost. I swear I'll be the first to get thrown out of a correctional home. Finally I have a goal for my life.

My destiny is in the balance because of a smashed nose on the beaten face of one of my brothers.

I can't cry, I can't cry for help, I can't ask for pity, or beg for mercy from Heaven. No one hears me, no one thinks of listening to me. There are two solutions: either I obey the system to my ultimate demise, until I'm reduced to a groveling slave, or I react against this injustice and lack of understanding, finally to be myself, so I can stop suffocating. I choose rebellion.

Can man change his fate? That's a subject for a baccalaureate in philosophy. For a child with no family, the question doesn't even come up. He answers with his life, his rage, his despair. And he changes his fate.

In hard times, daring to be different is like skiing a slalom under an avalanche ridge: either you get by or you get broken. For someone who doesn't count in anyone else's eyes, there's no getting aggravated when he falls. He doesn't lament his fate, he doesn't start crying. He gets up and keeps going, filled with a new rush of violence.

I'm sick of lining up every morning and listening to names getting rattled off for incoming mail. I'm never on the list. So and so, a letter, so and so, a package, so and so, two letters... There are lots of us that never get called, and I've decided to quit dreaming, to stop believing in miracles. My mother vanished into the wilderness, my father disappeared. I'm a son to no one, period.

"Guénard, there's someone to see you!"

"Get out..."

"Guénard, I'm not kidding. There's someone to see you in the front room!"

All of a sudden my heart starts beating faster. Boom boom, boom boom! I know I've sworn off dreams so as not to be disappointed, but I want so much to believe that my mother's finally come back... There are times when misfortune is so great that you'd think it would help tip the balance of fate from time to time.

I push the door to the front room and see Papa Gabe. Not my father, not my mother, but my Papa Gabe, whose barn I burnt down. After six months of incarceration and separation, he hasn't forgotten me. I wasn't expecting this visit; I'm completely overwhelmed. I remember the silence between us, and the benevolent, worried look on my guardian-father's face. He blames himself for letting me go without defending me, for having given in to his wife. I can see it all in his sad eyes. He didn't adopt me for fear that my father or my mother would one day want me back, and now bitterly regrets his choice. Yes, I can see sadness and regret in his gaze. But it's too late, papa.

Alarmed at the dismal hallways and sinister looking instructors, he asks: "Are you alright?"

I answer: "Yeah, I'm alright."

What can I say? That in six months' time I've become a beast with a bite? That I miss taking spins on the tractor, working in the fields, making the rounds of the animals, steaming-hot soup, fits of laughter, the smell of thatch, the color of wheat, the complicity of happiness? It's both too far away and too near. Another world, a wealth of memories I don't dare touch for fear of collapsing. I have to lock the past away if I want to survive.

There's silence between us, tear-filled eyes. Short goodbyes. He hugs me, holding me against him.

"Will you come back to see me, Papa Gabe?"

"I'll come back, my li'l tyke, I'll come back."

He leaves. Deep within me, I know he won't be back. I don't blame him. He's more shaken than I am. What he's just glimpsed of my world must be an unbearable torture for this man who was once the architect of my pastoral bliss. I feel abandoned once again. Seeing his slightly hunched silhouette diminishing down the alley, I quietly thank him for the few months of happiness he gave me.

Thank you for your visit and for your heart, Papa Gabe. It's not your fault, you passed through my life too quickly. You passed through my childhood like a river, fertilizing the seeds that were hidden away under the crust of abandonment. Like a Gypsy, I hide this treasure away in my lost child's baggage. You gave me a taste of the happiness of being loved. That happiness was unjustly taken from me. As short as it was, your visit brought up in me those happy memories that I can no longer have. I surrounded myself with armor, and it's falling to pieces. My heart has been so deeply furrowed that I want to become insensitive to love. It causes too much suffering. The best way to keep from hurting is not to love. Is that possible, Papa Gabe?

The few days following this visit are agony. Behind my hardened façade, my whole being has crumbled. One night, I want to end the torture, the unbearable suffering. I steal some pills from the infirmary and swallow them so I'll stop living. I feel ill and start throwing up. That's what saved me, against my will. The house physician takes at look and me and says: "Stick out your tongue... Hey, nice throat infection!"

An infection, on top of everything else? Darned unlucky.

Disgusted with living in a world of rancor. A massive breach. Powerless to hold back the waves of resentment that wash over me. I'm mad at my mother for not coming to get me. I'm mad at this fallen father who left me so many scars, so many bad dreams that keep me from sleeping, and terrified reflexes—if an adult pulls a handkerchief from his pocket or makes the slightest unexpected movement, my hands go up to protect my face.

One afternoon, three false brothers trash the bathrooms. I'm immediately called to the director's office. He's sitting behind his big desk; I'm standing, still, at attention.

"What am I going to do with you? I was told you ransacked the toilets and the bathrooms."

That's untrue, totally untrue. Those bastards pointed the finger at me. I'm no rat. I let him accuse me, without saying a word.

"Guénard, when you've got a rotten apple that you can't throw out, you get it out of the way, you isolate it, you set it aside so it won't spoil the rest of them. If you don't shape up, the next time you step out of line, the next time there's a fight, we're going to lock you up with the dogs!

I leave the office thinking I'd love to give a medal to whoever gets around to beating this guy up one day. He's never spoken to me like a human being. He's never asked me a question from his heart, nothing but threats, warnings and punishments. He and his team like to make people cry. They relish the fear they inspire.

But fear leads either to a desire to get even, or to the paralysis of a hypocrite or a rat. For my part, I dream of nothing but revenge. In the hall, the three rats are talking with the instructor who thinks he's Charles Bronson. That bastard's in on it. They're making fun of me on my way by.

That evening, after dinner, they're looking to get into it. I let them have their fun and play the coward. I have no desire to wind up in a cage with the two German Shepherds. I find a shower and lock myself in with all my clothes on. For part of the night they keep trying to get my goat. Insults and humiliation. I want to go out there and pound them but I keep hearing the director's threats echoing in my head. Sitting like a beggar on the lip of the shower stall, I implore invisible powers, greater powers, to come help me and set this injustice right. Then silence comes and invades the night. No one comes to my defense. My head and my body can't stand this suffocating shell. The hatred is rising within me, bursting, exploding.

I leave the shower. I run to the bathroom and tear the wooden hangers off the wall where we keep the towels. In a fury I run into the dorm room, roaring. They're sleeping like logs, those bastards. I start beating them with the hangar, the way we used to beat the wheat at Papa Gabe's. They mocked me, they made fun of my "flat nose," of my "rat's ears," is that what they call me? I'll rearrange their faces. They start screaming, blood starts gushing, the sheets are black. The others are screaming out of fear in the dark, and I keep hitting and hitting like a madman. I'm reveling in this violence, in this vengeance. What a rush!

In the midst of my blows, I hear the instructors running down the hall. They'll be here in a second. I know I've gone too far. Too late to go back. I have to run, unless I want to live in a concentration camp guarded by wolves. All these images flit through my mind. I toss my makeshift bat, start skidding across the blood-soaked floor and careen down the stairs, four at a time. I bolt across the courtyard. In front of me is the perimeter wall. Twelve feet high, topped with barbed wire. No choice. Charge!

With a running start and a mad dash, that night, for the first time, I scaled the great wall. The fear of the dogs must have lit my afterburners. I manage to grab the barbed wire on top of the enclosure and pull myself up. The steel claws tear into my left hand. I slide between the wall and the barbed wire. It catches my leg and tears my skin. I force my way through. It's too late to go back.

On the other side of the wall, I find a well-situated phone pole—one I picked out months ago—to serve as a ladder. I'm on the ground, on the right side of freedom. I'm bleeding, but I don't hurt. I can only feel the burning fear that's twisting my stomach. And the rage, and the joy at having made it out. My heart's beating out of control.

I start running until I drop, just to get away from the correctional home. It must be four in the morning and the alarm sounded immediately.

I keep walking, without a plan, without a goal, in a flat countryside. I emerge from the night. Day breaks, imperceptibly, into a dirty, gray dawn. I'm kind of a mess. The skin on my hand is pulling, covered in dried blood, and my bloodied leg is burning.

I'm limping. I have no water to wash in. I piss on my hand to disinfect it. It stings. Then I roll it in the dust, the way wounded boars do.

La Rochelle is awakening. I watch and marvel as the princess arises. The people have hair of all different lengths, clothes of all different colors. They seem to be going wherever they want to go, without being forced, and even in different directions from one another. I'm overwhelmed with an exquisite sense of well-being. Since I need to share this delightful richness, I start speaking to someone in my heart, like a poet. I sing my freedom, I give thanks for this fullness and for this new world whose doors have opened before me like the monumental doors of a citadel.

On this August ninth, the first day of my escape, lying in the grass, I spend part of the night contemplating the year's most starlit sky. Shooting stars are the most beautiful birthday candles anyone could hope for. I start listing wishes, dreaming. Tonight, I'm twelve years old and this life—my cruel step-mother—has given me the gift of freedom.

Chapter 9

Age Twelve
Escape and Disgust

One of my brothers in exile told me one night, as we lay dreaming of escapes, of adventures and close calls in our dorm room at the correctional home, that Paris was enormous and that you could hide there.

I didn't forget.

So I get on the road. I start walking toward the capital, all the way from the province of Charente-Maritime. I make headway especially at night so as not to be spotted by the police, following the railroad tracks. I thought to myself: "The cops must not stop trains, so follow the tracks." Anytime I start hearing a rumble in the background, I dive into a ditch. My heart starts beating wildly. I let the screaming convoy go by as I catch my breath.

I've been feeding on fruit, berries, mushrooms—unaware that some of them can be deadly—elderberry seeds and, inadvertently, on some sort of wild pepper... Little by little, without even realizing it, I'm rediscovering the age-old survival skills of my ancestry that modern city life has yet to root out entirely.

With no map and no landmarks to go by, I'm just following my instinct. My only concern is finding water. Sucking on roots and plants isn't enough to quench my thirst. I'm suffering from dehydration, but I can't bring myself to knock on someone's door and ask for a glass of water. I look older than twelve, but there's still no hair on my chin. The request could seem odd to a discerning adult.

By the time I get to Tours, I've had it, I'm dying of thirst. I'm ready to drink the Loire River. I find a faucet on the outer wall of the zoo. I start guzzling like an animal. When you drink crap, you get sick! For several hours I end up twisting in pain. I survive the zoo water anyway… I decide to take up hitchhiking to speed up my ascent to the Great Hideout.

After two weeks on the run, I arrive at the huge city gates. Like every tourist, I recognize Paris by the Eiffel Tower that emerges, noble and haughty from the midst of this giant conglomeration. I fall instantly in love. The Lady Giraffe draws me in irresistibly. I make my way haphazardly toward her through the city streets.

Once I reach her base, I start eyeing her up and down, in disbelief, growing dizzy. In my amazement, I circle her several times. I catch myself speaking to her, whispering words of affection. I start walking backwards, head back, my gaze fixed on this towering mass with its interlacing structure creating something of a kaleidoscope effect, and bump into a German couple, lost in the same dreamy state under this rose window of sky and beams. I don't know why, since I hadn't asked for anything, but the man offers me some money. What a godsend! I've long since gone through the fifty francs I was given by a man on Oléron Island where I had treated myself to a little detour to see the sights. "In memory of my son… because he was also a traveler," he said in a melancholy voice.

In one leg of the tower is a lady selling passes to the top of Lady Giraffe's long neck. I buy a ticket and start my ascent with the elation of a lover on his way to meet his beloved. Each level gives me a new sense of wonder. I'm discovering the world, indulging in this new, intoxicating freedom far, so far from the miasma of a sullied childhood. I'm gaining some perspective on my life. I exult as I discover the Champs-de-Mars, the military academy and the Chaillot Palace with its water fountains.

From the second level, I take flight, like a gull, over the river, the bridges, the tiny streets and the thousands of houses in this beautiful city. At the top, I make the fascinating discovery of a world of ants and the intoxicating sense of dominating, ruling, gliding, of escaping my misery.

I don't want to leave my Lady. At closing time, I have to go back down. I decide to keep watch near her. Night overtakes the gardens. I lie down behind a bush, next to the second straight pillar, across from the Trocadéro. There's a gentle air about. I sleep happily beneath the windows of the most expensive apartments in Paris.

Rising early, I start walking aimlessly in the direction of the military academy, Latour Maubourg, and the Invalides, exploring every street, every alley, every passage, to etch in my mind all the ins and outs of what would become my territory. I find myself wandering the neighborhood for several days. The nights are getting colder and damper. I've got nothing but a red nylon shirt on and I'm shivering. It takes me five days to remember what an animal knows instinctively, something I learned from Simla when I'd fall asleep against her in the doghouse: get your head as close to your nuts as possible and breathe on them, like a heat-gathering foil.

After a few nights I start stepping out on Lady Giraffe. I'm too cold. Where can I find a roof? At nightfall, I sneak into a bike garage on Rapp Avenue. I sleep for a few hours, all curled up between the bike wheels. I can't stay on my feet. In the street, you're not allowed to sleep when you're tired, especially if you're a twelve-year-old vagrant.

I get run off several times by people coming to get their bikes. The nicer ones say: "What are you doing here, my boy?" From the more crass ones I get: "What the hell are you doing here, you little hoodlum?" No sense trying to explain or argue with them... I take off, my eyes half shut, and look for a new place to stay. Finally I discover another bike garage, on Général Camou Street. There's no travel guide when you need to live for free in the street.

With some experience I start noticing, after a few weeks, that people are done putting away their bikes or their mopeds around midnight, and that they start moving again around five in the morning. That leaves me five quiet hours to snooze.

Every night, as I fall asleep, I make a solemn vow that if ever I have a house of my own, there'll be rooms for those who don't have one.

I'm starving. At my age I can't beg for change. I learn to steal, out of necessity. The first time, my target is a milk bottle that's just been delivered to a grocery store on Grenelle Avenue. It's six in the morning. I can't decide. Like a young cat, I circle my prey, not daring to put a paw out. I'm too hungry. Suddenly, my mind's made up. I'm off. I swipe the bottle. As soon as I have it in hand, I feel as if every camera in Paris were trained on me. I take off running, my guts playing the castanets. A few minutes later, in the Swiss Village—its labyrinth of pedestrian alleys is perfect for ducking hot pursuits—I pop the top off my loot and start drinking. With beads of sweat on my forehead, I experience a feeling I had never known: subsiding fear. I'm flying high!

Starting today, I'm a petty thief. I steal at set times to get a regular dose of that strange sensation of fear in my stomach that adds a bit of spice to my life. I get hooked on adrenaline. Fear is an enemy and a family member. I take it in hand at eight-thirty in the morning, then at two in the afternoon, while the other kids are in school. I keep a tight street urchin schedule.

The ones that are lucky enough to have parents can say hi to them in the morning; they're greeted in the evening when they come home from school, even if it's by a nanny. There are even some, I hear, whose parents come and kiss them goodnight before they go to bed. In my bizarre childhood, my fear has come to replace my mother. She's faithful, always there when you need her, like a mother at home. Fear awaits me and I go find her whenever I decide. She teaches me to be observant and trains my memory. Without this drug, my life would be dismal, dull and repetitive. Since it lacks meaning, it at least needs spice.

Freedom comes at a high price.
At first you've got a movie running in your head, discovering unknown worlds, playing with forbidden things and with fear, you relish the fact that you don't live like others. Then the days go by. The dream becomes a reality. It's not rosy every day. You're hungry, thirsty and tired. You walk for hours, exhausted, having your fill of unattainable promises and the temptations of enticing storefronts. Bitterness starts seeping in imperceptibly in the face of all that you can't live and all that you can't have. You're always on the lookout for the police making their rounds. You don't trust anyone. You're always on alert. You get used to stealing and even your thievery loses its appeal. Your beloved fear doesn't turn you on the way she used to.

The fairytale starts turning into a nightmare. It's too late: you don't want to admit it to yourself; that would take courage. But mostly you can't stop the steady stream of days anymore, this string of aimless hours, this wandering that removes you further and further from the real world and that you're finally pursuing for one single reason: better to live in the hell of this jungle than to return to the correctional home.

I walk a lot. My legs are holding up. One of my favorite circuits is from Latour Maubourg to République and back. At nightfall I make my way into my beautiful vagabond's quarters, imagining, as I pass one of those luxurious hotels, that some rich man will walk out and see me, take me under his wing and invite me to share the delights of his suite. The days go by. As do the nights. The rich remain feasting in their radiant palaces as I get back to my garage, exhausted and weak. At the end of my rope...

Could my wish be coming true? On a bench at the Champ-de-Mars, an elegant man comes up and sits down next to me. He's tastefully dressed, looking sharp, a well-kept sixty years of age. He seems trustworthy. I speak to him from my heart, without hiding the fact that I'm a penniless runaway, and that I'm looking for odd jobs.

He says: "Young man, I've got just the thing. How would you like to make fifty francs?"

I jump at the opportunity.

"Follow me."

We get to Commerce Street and enter an old apartment building. Its worn look leads me to believe that my protector is going to offer me a job painting the place. We walk into a dimly lit apartment, and there the well-dressed man asks me to take my clothes off. I refuse. He puts a weapon to my head.

Paralyzed, I suffer his vile, unfathomable assault.

Here I am in the street with fifty francs in my hand and utterly disgusted. There's a chill in my whole being. I hurt all over. I want to clean myself, wash away this disgrace. Where can I hide? My heart is overflowing with tears. Despair enters my soul like a chilling mist. I can't see straight. I'm shivering from my misery. I start walking toward Passy. In the square a puppet show has drawn an audience. I sit down. I'm a stranger, absent before this green tent, in the midst of other children and their mothers. One of the puppets turns to me and says: "You're sad like me!"

I run away.

I'm twelve and a few months and I've just discovered man's perversion, the things he's capable of imagining to sully himself and degrade other human beings. I felt the claws of evil within me, searching me out. It went beyond my body, it wounded my soul, a secret garden within me that was still pure. I was taken and I couldn't call for help. And yet, from within, in the deepest part of me, where there are no more words, I did call for help. I cried to an all-powerful being to come free me from this horror.

He didn't come.

No one came.

Chapter 10

Age Thirteen
Holding Up Hookers

I've been deeply wounded by this rape. My notions of the world are shattered and I've become distrustful where I might once have been simply naïve. My confidence is weakened, shaken. I'm like a wild rose bush in need of pruning, covered with thorns. I'd like to find an adult, a tutor to help me grow. But now I'm afraid that all men are like my father, like sadistic instructors or like elegant rapists from ritzy neighborhoods. I see the world of adults as a floor that looks sturdy, but that's actually rotted through, infested with termites, with lies and vices.

I keep wandering. I have no choice.

A few weeks after the incident, two well-dressed young men come up to me on Rapp Avenue. They invite me to dinner in a restaurant on St. Dominique Street. I'm thinking "once bitten twice shy," nevertheless I accept their offer. No one rapes a child in a restaurant. You also can't turn down a meal when hunger's got your stomach in knots.

One thing's for sure, these guys aren't from the Legion of Honor.

I share some of my sob story with them. They say: "Little brother, you're not alone anymore. Come with us, we'll take care of you."

I'm wary, hesitant, trying to size them up. One of them isn't lying. I get the feeling he's straight up and honest. The other one… I leave with them.

They're renting an apartment on Latour Maubourg Boulevard. They show me to my room and say goodnight. They're sharing a room. I find that reassuring. I lock myself in anyway, although it's not my body they seem to be interested in. Finally! I get to sleep in a real bed, with nice-smelling sheets… It feels so good to stretch my legs out. For nearly a year I've been sleeping curled up in my bike garage!

The next morning my two guardian angels knock on the door and give me a gentle wake-up: "Get up, little brother!"

Regretfully, I leave my cozy nest and hop in a piping hot shower. Next comes a hearty breakfast. It's like Byzantium at Latour Maubourg! I start wondering what this day and my two, somewhat shady-looking mentors have in store for me.

"Come on, little brother, we're going to dress you up right!"

They take me to a fancy tailor in the neighborhood. This ultra-high class guy starts taking my measurements with a tape measure that seems to spring magically from his hand. Then he brings out a brand new, three-piece gray suit with white pinstripes, an immaculate shirt, cufflinks, a tie and a cashmere jacket that feels like silk. I give up my polo shirt that smells of sweat, my cruddy pants, and I turn into a pint-sized lord. They complete their little magic trick by giving me a beautiful pair of patent leather shoes and a classy haircut at some fancy salon. No one's ever touched my head that gently before.

My new friends, Jacquot and Pierrot, pay everything in cash. It doesn't surprise me anymore. The day zips by. You'd never recognize me! I'm staring at myself in the storefront windows and I can't believe my eyes. I look like an Englishman. I start walking in zigzags to avoid puddles. I especially don't want to smudge my fancy nobleman's shoes!

"O.K., little brother, it's time for a little tourism!" A taxi drops us off at Place Blanche. Are they treating me to an evening at the Folies Bergères? The wings of the Moulin Rouge are beating away in the night, and this hot, bright neighborhood is teeming with people. We make our way over to a large café on Jules Joffrin Avenue. Spotlights pierce the room's smoke-filled darkness. My two big brothers buy me a lemonade at the bar.

"Wait for us here, we've got a meeting to go to."

They're off to chat with a few other guys. I can make out some not-so-friendly mugs.

As the parley comes to a close, an hour later, we start making our way "home." I can't imagine what these guys do for a living, nor what kind of sauce I'm about to get cooked in. One thing's reassuring: they're not child molesters. I can sleep soundly.

The next afternoon, Jacquot hands me my first weapon, a revolver, patiently explaining how it comes apart and how to use it. So, they're definitely not in sales. It isn't until that night that I start understanding the ins and outs of my new life.

Around 10 pm, we head back to Place Blanche. On the sidewalk, they tell me what I have to do. "Little brother, you wait for us here. We're going upstairs to take care of business. It shouldn't take us more than five or ten minutes. If you see anyone come out running, light 'em up!"

I say "right," without thinking, holding the piece in the pocket of my cashmere jacket.

Then Jacquot and Pierrot—we call him "the Belgian"—head into an old apartment building. I wait in front of a nearby movie theatre, watching the entrance. A shady-looking guy comes up to me:

"Come with me, I'll buy you a ticket."

"I can't, I'm waiting for someone."

The bastard tries again. I say "no" without looking at him, so this chicken hawk starts flipping out:

"Split, you little twerp!" he yells. "You've got no business being here, or else you're coming with me to the movie!"

He grabs my arm and wants to drag me toward the lighted porch. I slip my hand in my pocket and, just as I'm about to stick my toy under his nose, Jacquot and Pierrot come flying out of the building.

"Run, little brother, follow us, quickly!"

Without understanding what's going on, I take off, leaving the queer dumbfounded.

We take off toward the metro, catch a passing subway and there we are, catching our breath on this rumbling old train. Standing in a corner, Pierrot smiles at me and motions for me to come over. He opens his coat with a laugh and shows me the butt of his pistol. It's bloody.

"Look here, little brother," he whispers, tapping his leg.

Peering into a wide pocket, I see rolls of bills, lots of money.

"See, it's pretty quick," he says, with a wink.

I reach for the railing to keep from falling over. I'm dizzy, my head spinning like a merry-go-round, I go weak in the knees. I can guess where the dough came from and what kind of business my bros are involved in. They hold up hookers. The bills the Belgian's got are the earnings of a woman from Pigalle and the black juice on his gun is her blood. Her skull must be in pretty bad shape. I feel sorry for the girl they just beat up.

Every once in a while, when I'm wandering the streets and come across one of these sisters of the night, I think to myself that one day I'll either marry a virgin or a prostitute. I don't like what's in between. I often stop to talk with these women peddling their charm. We share the habit of wandering the sidewalks. We chat on the beat and I sense their mothering heart awakening at hearing all my trials. These street girls are understanding and gentle with me. Some of them offer me money, and even a place to stay. I've fallen in love with these night-birds, entangled in their fishnet stockings. So many of them have the heart of a princess.

Most of them are country girls who came to the city dreaming of Prince Charming. They quickly descended into Hell at the hands of an unscrupulous slave runner. Some have a child or two that they've left back home, in the care of their grandparents. They have a chance to visit them only once a month. The pimps use the little ones as insurance.

"If you don't come back, I'll pop your kid," the bastards say. "Or else I'll tell him and the rest of your family about all of your lovely Parisian ways!"

These poor girls are prisoners of their reputation. They show up to give their kids a quick kiss and make up a story to explain their absence, or else they just wall themselves off in silence, then return to their sidewalks with shattered hearts. The rebels and the runaways are sent North of Barbès, to the discount lines for immigrant workers. A hundred or so encounters a day destroy both their bodies and their souls.

And here I am, being an accomplice in holding up hookers.

I'm also just realizing that I nearly took out the queer. If Jacquot and the Belgian hadn't come out when they did, would I have popped him? Maybe...a few seconds later and my whole life could have been in the balance.

Jacquot isn't saying anything. I wonder if he can guess my state of mind, sitting over there in his jump seat. He's giving me a calm, pensive look, then takes me by the shoulder: "Say, little brother, after all that emotion we're going to go take a breather at Mario's. We've earned that much."

Mario's is an Italian restaurant in the 18th district. Seated at the tables are lots of Latin-looking men, well-dressed, their hair slicked back, with gold chains around their necks. The kind of guys you wouldn't want to mess with. They're talking "business." If someone told me this was the Mafia's mess hall, I wouldn't bet against them. Mario, the boss, a big, burly, jovial kind of guy, shakes my hand and says: "Have a seat here, kid."

He's very paternal, that Mario. We're in a dimly lit, smoke-filled back room. A low-hanging lamp is lighting a billiards table, surrounded by five smaller tables. On the far, windowless wall, is an enormous mirror, a bench made of Havana leather, a large table and a few brown, wooden chairs.

Mario leans toward Jacquot, and pointing towards me asks: "Is that your brother?"

Jacquot pulls my tie and says yes with a wink.

"You're putting him on the payroll kind of early, don't you think?" asks the boss.

Silence. Pierrot is playing with his knife. It's a large switchblade. He keeps fidgeting, couldn't be more nervous. His reactions are unpredictable. Mario keeps talking to Jacquot, and not to Pierrot. The boss breaks the silence and starts talking again, as if nothing were going on: "I have a job in the area of Sarthe. Should be good, easy and guaranteed juicy. It ought to pay off pretty big."

He starts rubbing his fingers together and gets up, inviting Jacquot to follow him. Pierrot moves to go with them, but Mario waves him back to his seat.

"Hey, the Belgian guy stays here, and don't let my spaghetti get cold!"

Pierrot starts gritting his teeth, obviously furious. The tension is mounting. A sinister looking server fills his plate without taking his eyes off him. Pierrot stares back at him. A second later he's unrecognizable, turns into a wild beast and pounces on the server.

From their seats at a nearby table, Jacquot and Mario come running over and separate the two men struggling on the ground. Pierrot starts spewing curses. Jacquot raises his voice: "That's enough, sit down, eat and zip it!"

Pierrot obeys. He retreats into a seething silence.

Mario sits down to have dinner with us. He's very considerate of Jacquot and me, but his look changes as soon as he sees Pierrot. I can tell he doesn't trust him and holds some secret animosity toward him.

The pasta is delicious and Mario offers me a second dessert. When it's time to leave, he gives me an affectionate pat on the head and whispers in my ear: "Whatever you do, kid, only listen to Jacquot, you can only trust Jacquot!"

We cross the main dining area. The server behind the bar is glaring at us on our way out, a stern look on his face. Jacquot is keeping a hand on Pierrot's arm. There's a stormy atmosphere hovering. Out in the street, Pierrot blows up. He slaps me hard saying: "What did he say to you before we left, you little brat? Huh, what did he say to you?"

Jacquot grabs him by his lapels, gets up in his face and screams: "You touch this kid and I'll kill you! Don't ever do that again!"

The trip home is weighed down with about three tons of silence. I'm scared of Pierrot. He exudes violence and nastiness. Jacquot is nice to me, almost like a brother. That man's got a heart.

While Jacquot is in the shower, Pierrot calls me over to him. He pulls out his gun and puts it up to my head.

"You little shit, I'm going to roast your brain!"

I close my eyes, he's going to shoot, the bullet's going to put a hole in my skull and send me off into the night. This guy's a lunatic, he could do anything. He pulls the trigger. It's the end. Click. He busts out laughing: "Ha, ha! I got you, you little shit! Scared the crap out of you, didn't I?"

He grows serious again and stares at me: "See, if you screw around, I'll put a hole in you. Next time there'll be a bullet!"

He takes off.

The air is heavy, tension is growing. Jacquot comes back and asks me: "Did you like the evening, little brother?"

I answer yes, quietly.

"Mario likes you, you know. He says you've got the look and the build of a chief. You've still got a lot to learn: obeying without asking questions and trusting only one man. By the way, what did Mario tell you?"

"To follow and listen only to you."

"Don't mind Pierrot. He's uptight because he's AWOL from the Foreign Legion. He's a good soldier, a bit cracked.

I head to bed, still a bit uneasy. Jacquot was reassuring but my sleep is about as smooth as a lake on a stormy night. Images of blood, bills, fights, frantic escapes and broken skulls are all mixed together in my dreams along with the affectionate look on Mario's face, basil pasta and creamy desserts.

The next day, I'm walking along in the neighborhood when someone taps me on the shoulder. It's Pierrot. He's eyeing me with an expression full of scorn and anger. He looks around, opens his jacket, pulls out his gun tipped with a silencer and aims it at a streetlight about thirty meters away. Pop! The bulb explodes. The Belgian puts his gear away and says: "I'll put a hole in you, you little shit!"

He turns and spits as he walks away. Everything just got bumped up a notch.

Chapter 11

Age Fourteen
Playing the Gigolo at Montparnasse

Early one afternoon, Jacquot takes me to La Coupole, the famous Montparnasse café. I'm alone with him. I don't know where the Belgian's gone off to, but I feel better without him there. This morning, Jacquot bought me some fancy new clothes and a pair of patent leather shoes. We take a seat on one of the benches of the huge hall and order an orange soda. Jacquot starts explaining:

"Listen, here's the drill. You'll come here, have some tea and read a newspaper. You'll do it exactly the way I tell you. You'll order a second cup of tea, then ask for the bill. If the server says it's been paid, discretely ask him who took care of it. You'll fold your paper and walk over to the woman he points out to you, thanking him with a nod. You'll walk slowly toward the exit, hold the door open for the woman, step aside and smile as you let her through. You'll accompany her to her car and get in with her. Got it?"

I answer yes and repeat the different steps of the operation. Actually, I don't get any of it. What's the point of this drill? I feel like I'm playing the part of a secret agent who never quite got his mission.

Why does Jacquot want me to get into her car with her? I'm having a hard time following his little soap opera, but I don't dare ask him any questions.

The next day, a Friday afternoon, I head back to La Coupole with a lump in my stomach. Seeing the number of women sitting around, I quickly pick up the fact that I'm not a secret agent. Jacquot is sitting about twenty meters away. He's acting like he doesn't know me. I order some tea. I open my newspaper. The pages slide out, fall to the floor and get crumpled. I try gathering the huge pages and putting them back in order. It's a delicate procedure when you've got to hold it upright. The paper's mocking me. I should have practiced in my room at the house. I must look ridiculous, and I imagine everyone staring at me and sniggering. I turn beet-red. I forget to look up at the women. I down one cup of tea, then a second, then a third, a fourth, and I can't bring myself to ask who's picking up the tab. I need to pee really badly, but I can't get up. I start squeezing my legs tighter and tighter together. After my fifth cup of tea, I'm about to explode, so I zip to the end of the hallway and to the left.

Jacquot meets me in the bathroom. He's mega-pissed.

"What the hell are you doing?"

"Well, uh, look, I'm going pee..."

"Yeah, I can see that. What else?"

He's mad. I don't dare tell him I'm intimidated.

"Uh, well, it's the newspaper, see... I don't really have that part down. I probably should have taken a smaller one.

"Who the hell cares about the paper!? Alright, that's enough, just go back and sit down and ask for the bill!"

Sheepishly, I head back to my seat. The server brings me a sixth cup of tea. I hadn't ordered anything and I'm getting pretty tired of this insipid brew, even if I do look like Englishman in my new suit. The server says: "It's from the lady, over there."

I smile at him, I smile at her. Nice surprise, it's a beautiful woman, around fifty years of age, blond with a well-kept figure.

I lucked out. I could have wound up with an old, ugly hag.

In a dignified manner, I get up, walk toward her, greet her. She smiles. I walk straight toward the door and hold it open for her, then follow her to her car. It's a Cadillac. As I climb in beside her, I find myself beginning to enjoy this ceremony.

"Home, Roger!" she says to the chauffeur.

The twenty-minute drive, spent in silence, leads us to a sumptuous house located in a western suburb of Paris.

From there, I just go with the flow...

The weekend turns out to be thoroughly enjoyable. This woman, looking for a gentle touch, introduces me to a tenderness I had never known, spoiling me like a son, like a lover.

On Monday morning, her chauffeur drops me off in Paris after handing me two thousand francs. That comes out to about two months' salary. The current minimum wage is around eight hundred francs.

To tell the truth, I can't say I disliked my first foray into prostitution. I give Jacquot the money. With a wink he tosses me two hundred francs: "See, it's a snap!" True, it is easy, it pays well and I'd much rather give some love to a lonely woman than shake down the prostitutes I like so much.

Unfortunately, the one doesn't rule out the other.

I would spend a year in this three-beat rhythm: hold-ups on week nights; glam weekends with four regular clients; and miserably empty days. The money's pouring in, but happiness doesn't come with it. The days seem long, and I envy the kids that are in school while I practice disassembling and reassembling my gun with my eyes closed, and drawing as fast as possible. Jacquot takes good care of me. He's an adopted brother. He's not a father.

As I draw my gun, sometimes I see my father's silhouette in the mirror. Do I shoot, do I not shoot? I think I want him to suffer a bit before I shoot.

I spend my recesses in the street, when classes let out, watching every affectionate gesture of parents for their children: one hand taken in another, a pat on the cheek, kisses on the neck, foreheads and noses rubbing together... These signs of tenderness are like splinters in my heart. I imitate them and repeat them with my clients, with these mature women that I'm learning to understand, to pity and to love. They're lonely, tragically lonely in their golden palaces, their luxurious cages, maintained by husbands whose zippers are as active as their wallets. Husbands who leave them for some spring chicken they keep in a bachelor pad, or take with them on weekends to Saint-Tropez or Megève.

I have a thirst for affection and find myself enjoying both receiving and giving it. The weekends are a kind of gentle isolation that lets me forget my loneliness and the hold-ups that are starting to weigh on me more and more. Jacquot and Pierrot are moving me up in the ranks, but I'd just as soon do without. I'm not just their lookout anymore, I've become an active member of the gang. On the sidewalk I ask the girls their rates and negotiate as if I were some wet-behind-the-ears kid looking for a chick. We go upstairs, she's not on her guard. Jacquot follows me in the shadows. He jumps in before the exchange while Pierrot keeps an eye out below, or vice versa.

It's a dangerous game. The pimps are never far away. You can never tell how the girls are going to react. Some are desperate, they couldn't care less about the threat of a gun and start screaming. Others are drunk and start hitting. There have been fights, shots fired, blood, and I'm thinking my two brothers are going too far. We try different neighborhoods, but now our racket's been made. The pimps and the girls are on the alert. We switch roles, just to change things up a bit... Something bad's going to happen. On several occasions we wind up with bullets zipping by our heads. The lure of money, the catch of always wanting more and the adrenaline rush all tend to dull common sense and caution.

Once in a while, during a scuffle, I'm struck with a longing for death. A flash of despair. I hope for a stray bullet. This life is pointless. There's no way out. I can't stand being a part of these girls' suffering anymore. I wouldn't mind gunning down the pimps, though. But mostly, I can't stand Pierrot's gratuitous violence. He has to start hitting every time, even if the girl gives up and hands over her cash without complaining. The sadistic bastard gets off on it and I want to make him pay.

When we can, we hit up the girls whose pimps got landed in the hospital. We set up a parallel circuit that brings in more for the hooker: half for us, half for her. By the time her pimp gets back, she's put some money away.

Premonition, or intuition? I can sense that Jacquot is fed up with it too. He can't stand the Belgian and trusts him less and less. He feels sorry for most of our victims. He's even moved up the time for our visits—we start around 10 pm—so they can have time to make some of it up before the night's out. Our income's going down—there's not much to grab at that time of night—and Pierrot's mad as can be.

To settle him down, we go rough up the queers at the Trocadéro or at the Tuileries. Jacquot turns out to be far less gentle than he is with the girls. We've got a pretty good system worked out: I get in the car, pretending to be looking for some action. Once I've got the queer's trust, I grab the keys from the ignition. Jacquot and Pierrot make their move to his window and show him their kind of charity. I get off on beating them up. It's like getting a bit of revenge for what was done to me.

It soothes my memory.

That circus keeps up every day, except for the weekends when I'm the hooker for the rich women of La Coupole.

On Friday afternoons, Jacquot says with a laugh: "It's time for you to go take care of business with the ladies."

All I'd ever known about women was the wound of my mother's abandonment and the harshness of some teachers. Through the care of these ladies, I discover a little sweetness and gentleness.

One day, one of them takes me in her arms, caresses my cheek and whispers that famous line: "You know, you've got pretty eyes!" She said it from her heart. It's the first time a woman's ever paid me such a wonderful compliment.

I'm fourteen. She's not my mother…

Chapter 12

The Train Station, My Big Brother Takes Off

One Monday morning in November, I get back to Latour Maubourg after a weekend in good, sweet company, with twenty-five hundred francs in my pocket. I'm looking forward to seeing Jacquot.

I ring the doorbell, no one answers. I knock, no luck. I start pounding on the door and calling out. No response. I wait until noon, sitting in the stairwell. No Jacquot, no Pierrot. I head over to Lucien's, a restaurant we go to for lunch from time to time. No one's seen them. I find that odd, I'm starting to panic.

That afternoon I run over to Mario's. He's out. This is getting weirder and weirder. I start walking from Jules Joffrin to Latour Maubourg, suddenly feeling the same loneliness that so marked my first weeks in Paris. I'm also getting worried. There's still no one at the apartment. Returning to Mario's, I'm relieved to find him there. He seems relieved as well and smiles as he walks over to me.

"Hey, there you are, little guy! I'm glad to see you. They told me you came by this afternoon. Come and sit down, you and I need to talk."

We find ourselves a seat in the billiards room and he signals the others to leave us alone.

"Would you like something to drink?"

"Yes sir, thank you."

"When are you going to start calling me Mario?"

While I'm emptying my glass, he says:

"You're looking for your brother and that other ass, aren't you? They botched a job... All because of the Belgian. I told your brother not to hook up with a deserter. A bad soldier stays bad... He didn't listen."

Mario grows silent, furrows his brow. He looks worried. I'm dying to hear some news of Jacquot, but I don't dare ask him. Is he still alive? Did he get arrested?

As if he were guessing my silent questioning, Mario continues: "Don't worry, your brother's safe and sound. He's on his way. He's alive. He's going to have to lay low for a while, until everybody forgets about him. As for you, little guy, you've got your whole life to build a good business. Take advantage of this incident to change your course. You're too young for the kind of business you're in now, it'll end up badly. Don't waste the best years of your life. Look at my son; he's your age and living quietly with his mother and his sisters. Go back to your parents, live the good life!"

Mario talks about taking a break, laying low, being like his son... I'd like nothing more than to live with my father and mother. Why not both at the same time while we're at it?! The lump in my throat is growing. I'm nobody's son. My whole life I've been on the run. Change my course? And go where? You can never rest when you're on the lam, especially when you're fourteen.

From within my child's prison I dreamt of freedom, but in the streets all I found was worry and loneliness, grotesque violence beneath the hypocrisy of a proffered hand—the law of the jungle. Kind Mario has sent me unwillingly, even unwittingly, back to my original pain. His words have torn open the scars of my memories. The wound is suddenly wide open. It's oozing a long-festering rage. No, I don't want to be an abandoned child!

At the correctional home, I was called a "bad seed" often enough. Children are like mustard seeds, or grains of wheat. If they don't grow up well or abundantly, it's because they weren't cared for. You can't ask them to love what's beautiful, true and good when they haven't been guided toward what's beautiful, true and good. You can't ask them to believe in mankind when no one was ever there to wait for them or to listen to them. For a seed to bear fruit, you have to care for the ground around it with love, you have to watch its growth, prune from time to time, weed often, and you have to respect its time.

I leave Mario after dinner with all these ideas spinning around in my head, without saying a word. He drops me off at Invalides. Before we separate, he whispers: "Hey kid, don't ask your brother too many questions. Tell him I'll meet him at Lucien's tomorrow at noon."

I run all the way to Latour Maubourg and climb the stairs four at a time. Arriving on the second floor, I knock, I ring the doorbell. Jacquot opens the door.

"Come on in, little guy, where were you?"

I just want to hug him. He's my big brother and I was so afraid for him. I'm out of breath, more from all the emotion than from running, but I manage: "With Mario... he said... to tell you... tomorrow at noon... at Lucien's."

"OK, Mario's doing alright, good. You're alright, good. Well, you see, for me things aren't so good, little brother."

I keep quiet. I'm afraid of what's coming next. I try to make myself small and hide in a corner before this fallen hero.

"You see, little brother, I'm out. I've made enough dough and I don't want to spend the rest of my life walking in the shadows. You won't ever see the other bastard anymore, you won't be afraid anymore and he's not going to pop you... He screwed up, he didn't do what I told him and wound up on the slab."

Jacquot's got his head in his hands, he's white as a ghost, gaunt and sad. I've never seen him so bent out of shape. Suddenly, he gets up, grabs his three guns and puts his hand out.

"Give me yours."

I hand him my pistol. He wraps the weapons in some newspaper, some rags and some string and tapes the whole bundle together.

"I'm quitting everything. I'm going away with the girl you saw the other day. She's got me under her skin. She wants to get married. She's beautiful and she's loaded, and that can't hurt. I'm sorry, little brother, we're about to go down separate paths. I'm giving you back your freedom. Tomorrow, you've got to fend for yourself. Leave this business, find a sensible job. You're resourceful, you're a go-getter, you'll make it.

We turn in, following those awful words. I can't begin to sleep. I don't want to leave Jacquot. He's my big brother. He protects me, he covers for me. We share the risks and the loot. Sure, he gets paid more, but I don't hold that against him, he's older than I am. The next morning, I open my eyes to find Jacquot all dressed up. His new life is starting off with a bang, mine with depression. We each take our suitcases in hand and slam the door on the apartment where we shared a year of our lives and countless emotions. I accompany him on the subway all the way to the Gare du Nord.

On the outbound platform, he stops, looks at me for a long time, takes me in his arms and says: "Thank you, little brother. You were my first little brother, the one I'd always wanted."

Tears are gleaming in his eyes. He boards the train for Brussels. I take off so I won't start crying in front of him. My knees are knocking, my heart and my throat are all knotted up, I'm suffocating from the pain. Within me, the floodgates are thrown open, letting the great waters of sorrow flow like Niagra Falls. I start wandering, my suitcase in hand. I'm going in circles. I come back to the train station, drawn to this platform by the foolish hope that my beloved brother suddenly changed his mind and got off the train. No, the platform is empty, the train is gone and Jacquot with it. He's gone from my life and I have to chase him out if I want to keep from hurting.

No sooner do I put my suitcase in safe keeping than two on-duty officers ask me for my papers. With all the emotion, I had let my guard down. I forgot about those guys... I start going through my pockets trying to think of the best way to get myself out this tight spot. A group of Dutch tourists emerges from a platform right behind the cops; they're distracted for a second. That's my cue. I bump one of them, roll to the ground and get up in the midst of these befuddled tourists who slow the officers in their pursuit. I take off running across the station. I'm outside, in the street, running like a madman, my nose stinging from the cold. I don't hear any shots or whistles, and no one's running after me. Whew! I lost them. Where to now? Jacquot asked me never to go back to the apartment, or to any of the places we used to hang around together.

At fourteen, how am I supposed to survive the great, lonely city, especially with winter on the way?

Chapter 13

Age Fifteen
Around the World with Monsieur Léon

Alone again.

Reluctantly, I start rediscovering my old habits and find a bike garage to sleep in, near Bir-Hakeim, on Alexandre Cabanel Street. I'm having the hardest time falling asleep. The rich man's habits I developed in Jacquot's cushy apartment have made me rather susceptible to discomfort and cold weather. In this two by three meter storage space, crammed with bikes, where there's no room to stretch out, I find myself shivering, both from the cold and from sadness.

The next day, I'm on the move. It's getting colder and colder. Jacquot left me some money, but it's not going to be enough to get me through the winter. I've got to find some work, most of all to keep my mind busy. My brain's been on overdrive ever since my big brother left.

I approach a man near the Champ-de-Mars, as politely as humanly possible, thanks to the expressions I learned from my clients at La Coupole. A terrible memory is coming back to me. I've got no choice. This man seems very proper. I tell him my troubles and that I'm looking for work. He listens attentively then, with some reassuring words, asks me to follow him: "My boy, I'm going to introduce you to an acquaintance. He may have a job for you."

Here we are in front of a grocery store on Saint-Dominique Street. My mentor seems to have a good reputation around here; the boss at the store greets him respectfully. He introduces me as a trustworthy young man, a hard worker. He gives me such a good recommendation that the boss hires me on the spot. When asked for my papers, I reply: “No problem, I’m sixteen, I’ll be sure to bring them tomorrow.”

Naturally, the next day I forget to bring the papers I don’t have and I start working. It’s tough. Large wooden crates, full of wine or lemonade bottles, need to be unloaded. They’re heavy, really heavy. A strong guy from Martinique is tossing me these crates and I have to catch them on the fly. This hulking brute is laughing: “Is that silly-string or spaghetti you’ve got in those arms?”

I don’t respond, I check my temper to keep from sending my spaghetti into his face. I’m fighting with the crates and they’re cutting into my arms; all these bottles of wine have to be moved to the cellar. I need this job and I don’t want to disappoint the man who helped me get it, it’s a question of honor. At the end of this first day, I’m worn out, my arms are tattered and I’m proud of myself. I earned my wages, even if they are a mere pittance compared to my income from the weekend.

I grab a bonus. Not too legit. Well, at least it’s less dishonest than robbing hookers. I abscond with some sliced turkey and some coffee and slide the bundle through the basement window in the storage room. It opens onto an adjacent street. As I leave work, I make my way around the building, kneel by the window to tie my shoelace and pick up my dinner for the evening. Sitting on a bench at Löwendal Square, I enjoy my dinner, tearing into the raw meat like the lion roaring on his rock in the middle of this garden. For dessert I start sucking on the coffee beans.

The next morning, the boss sets me up selling fruits and vegetables. I learn to weigh, to wrap and to find just the right words for the customers. One kind little word that brightens their day along with a sunny smile. I always put a little extra in the bag after weighing it. People notice that kind of attention. The days go by and winter settles in, not too gray, not too sad. The regulars talk to me nicely. These good people would never guess that I'm a runaway who sleeps in their basements and gets a bath only once a week at the municipal swimming pool.

One day I deliver a bag of groceries to a woman who gives me an enormous tip. She smiles at me with the radiant smile of a princess. She's classy, elegant, confident, and she's got a raspy voice. I'm completely taken. I ask the concierge what she does for a living. He looks at me as if I had a screw loose: "Well, that's Jeanne Moreau!"

"...? Who's Jeanne... Boreau?"

"You know, the actress!"

I have no idea who this Jeanne Moreau is, but her tip just gave me an idea. I start doing some work on the side, deliveries during lunch breaks and in the evening, after work. I start saving up. The boss likes me:

"If you keep this up, by the time you're twenty-one, you'll have your own shop. Don't forget to bring me your papers tomorrow. You've been saying you would for the last six months..."

I get myself out of that confrontation thanks to a change in management. I tell the new guy I showed them to the old guy and it's all taken care of.

On Saturday nights and Sundays, I keep on entertaining some of the more privileged clients from La Coupole. I'm starting to get overworked.

After a few months, an observant customer guesses that I don't have a home. Maybe it's the smell? But I douse myself with deodorant... The man in question is ageless, not all that clean either. He offers me a place to stay. It's a godsend. I'm tired of the hide-and-sleep routine in the bike garage. I've collected enough money to get a hotel room or to rent a place, but I'm too young and I'd get nabbed right away.

The man is a caretaker at a large bookstore on Latour Maubourg Boulevard. I find him strange. His place is small, damp and noisy. My suspicion is confirmed. On the very first night, this homo proposes some "things": firmly rejecting his advances, I start getting ready to leave, but he invites me to stay regardless. Although he respects me, his disturbing presence makes for some troubled sleep.

I would spend several months in his lair, in a pad that wreaked of vice, carefully watching my comings and goings to avoid being seen by anyone else in the building. My work has helped me integrate the neighborhood. I greet passers-by like old acquaintances; the cops think I'm just a local kid.

But you never know... the fear of being sent back to the correctional home keeps me on my toes. I take some precautions. For instance, I've developed the habit of noting the names of every street I walk down. If I get stopped, I just say that I live right nearby, at number such and such, on so and so street, with my grandmother or my mother, Mrs. so and so. I recite the name by heart and the number. It works, the cops believe me. I don't pour it on. If they get suspicious and want to take me home to check, there's only one thing left to do: hightail it and lose them in a hurry.

There's nothing like tricking the guys that are after you! Like coming out of the catacombs after getting lost for hours in a dark, underground maze. It's the spice of my life! I'm learning to control my breathing when I hide behind the door of a courtyard or under a car whenever a patrol's tailing me. I wonder if the pounding of my heart could give me away?... My beloved fear remains faithful.

I spend my evenings wandering the city streets, stealing with a glance the happiness of lovers, of children and their parents, of all those who love each other and don't try to hide it. Like a lone eagle, I observe, I watch, I pick out a prey and don't let go. And yet I come away without a father, without a mother, without happiness and without love... with nothing but painful images.

Every night, in the balcony overlooking life's theater, I watch intently the people on the verandas of local pubs, in line at the movies and behind restaurant windows. Every night, my actors change. Every night, the play's scenario is repeated over a background of laughter, joy, winks, interlaced fingers and joined lips. Every night, my solitude lays another furrow.

Some nights, in the Latin Quarter, when I find myself following the tender meanderings of these happy strollers, it's more than I can take. I walk toward the two lovers holding hands and make a disruptive pass between them to break the symbolic bond of their love. Their presence is overwhelming, setting off within me an uncontrollable storm whose bolts of lightning are immediately directed at my father. I'm drowning in waves of hatred. My fists tighten in my pockets.

At times, when I'm sneaking back into my apartment building, I'll pass a boy who's just given in to the concierge's advances. It makes me want to puke and beat the crap out of that pervert. I'd rather run away. Worn out by my nocturnal escapades, I head back to my bike garage to try and get some sleep. Sickening images keep washing over me.

The next morning I'm far from tip-top shape for work. I try to hide my fatigue.

"Hey, Philip, were you out partying last night?" asks the manager with a laugh.

If only he knew... I start silently cursing myself out, just to keep myself going: "Come on, you weakling, you're losing it, let's go, suck it up!"

One day the boss calls on me:

"A delivery for the radio station, Jacques Picard studio."

Guénard assures a timely service, it's like it was already there.

Arriving at the Jacques Picard studio, I nearly drop my package. My customers are four singers with moustaches. The James Brothers in person! They're rehearsing. I pour them a drink and just stand there listening, fascinated by the kindness, talent and professionalism of these generous artists. To think I'd been looking for things to get my butt in gear. This is huge, seeing these guys starting their song over seven times: "I've got some jam...," along with all the amusing expressions that follow because they're not happy with the results. A swift kick in the behind is what this is! I'm wide awake now.

I head back to the shop happy and feeling flattered.

"Gee, Guénard, you sure took your time! What did you do, take drinks to the entire staff?"

The boss laughs. He's kind. I tell him my story and, like an accomplice, he starts sending me regularly on deliveries to the studios. I meet different artists there and wind up with a few rehearsal shirts from Johnny Halliday and Dick Rivers. I'm on cloud nine every time I come out of there. Here I am, nobody's son, and I'm catering to the stars...

After such wonderful days, I stay in my bike garage, or in the squalid quarters of the old pervert, and dream that one of these artists is eventually going to look at me, notice me, take a liking to me, invite me to stay with him and share a part of his gilded world. You dream any way you can. Dreaming takes time away from the misery, the suffering and the anguish. It's a trip that costs little and bothers no one. And the dream train never goes on strike...

I like these artists. Not because they're popular, but for what they are: strong and fragile. When I look at them, I feel as if I could pass beyond the window dressing of fame and slide backstage, into their hearts, catching an intimate glimpse into their secret abodes.

I serve them drinks without a word, without pestering them for autographs. I'm at their service. For the most part, the rehearsals are tedious. They'll start a song over from the top for a glitch the average listener would never pick out. It pains me to see their efforts come to a halt. Some obey without a word; others curse and complain; others laugh it off; then there are those ultra-sensitive ones who take the interruption as a failure or an insult. They seem to be right on the edge. My admiration is boundless.

All this work, all this effort, culminating in the Big Night, in the magical and sacred moment when the artist steps out on the stage with butterflies in his stomach, blinded by the spotlights, facing an eager and demanding crowd. They're magnificent and alone, ready to give it their all, like a star rising at dusk.

These dreams follow me through chaotic nights in my bike palaces. I opted to leave the gay concierge's place before turning him into ground beef. I can't take seeing him luring young prey into his fetid lair and perverting them.

I like wandering the posh neighborhoods—they're posh, which helps when you're feeling the dreariness of solitude. One evening while I'm meandering through the neighborhood of Auteuil, I come across an odd sort of fellow. He calls himself Léon and sits on a sidewalk bench as if he were on a throne. He says to me: "Young man, do you know where Honduras is located?"

Did I hear that correctly? Is he asking for some information?

"Honda what?"

"Honduras, young man?"

"Is that a subway stop?"

"No, young man, it's neither a subway stop nor the name of the next winner of the Triple Crown."

"Is Hon... der... us a country?"

"Bravo, young man! Honduras is indeed a country. We're making some progress..."

Amazing fellow! His demeanor is dignified, even noble, and belies the wear of his clothing. The cashmere coat he's wearing is so threadbare it's colorless and his shoes are as worn as his vest is thin. Everything about this man is in tatters. Even his fine, distinguished features are sagging. Monsieur Léon is homeless and he reads the *Times*. It's rarely current, but he's less worried about getting news late than about not getting it at all.

"They're bound to be delayed a little. So what's a little sooner or later when you're talking days...? And then stepping back and getting a little perspective on events never hurts!"

I soon find myself very attached to Monsieur Léon, a man who, under his tired appearance, is hiding a deeply noble soul and a tremendous heartache. This man bears the wounds of a life that took his wife and their only son in a car accident for which he continues to blame himself. His whole life came crashing down when he lost his only loves. Stripped of his soul, he slowly lost interest in living what had been a respectable life. He left his job at the Paris Stock Exchange, gave up his high-powered socializing and even some family ties that he felt others were only maintaining out of self-interest. What was the point of earning a living when life had lost its meaning? Monsieur Léon let himself drift little by little into a quiet, liminal state. His homelessness severed his last connections to his family.

I find Monsieur Léon intriguing. I go to see him nearly every day.

His French is impeccable and his culture immense. He shares his knowledge eloquently, pleased to have found an attentive ear and an affectionate gaze. He's a five star bum! He claims he sleeps in a palace near Porte d'Auteuil. One day he finally accepts to satisfy my curiosity:

"You want to see my palace, young man? Well then, let's go!"

He takes me to see his Hilton: an abandoned railcar at the Auteuil train station.

Every evening Monsieur Léon gives me an overview of the day's news, with a touch of humor and his critical commentary. Together we travel around the world, from Singapore to Honduras.

With him I don't even try to bluff, I readily admit my extreme ignorance. He laughs and says: "Young man, allow me to further your geographical education."

From his breast pocket he pulls an old notebook with worn pages, out of which he draws a world map that he unfolds as if it were the map to a hidden treasure. Pointing to a tiny spot between North and South America he says: "Young man, here's Honduras, don't ever forget it!"

The former financier begins teaching me about the Stock Exchange. My tutor and I—a child without a school—invest imaginary fortunes in actual stocks. Monsieur Léon evaluates their progress while giving me lessons in geopolitics, on the colonial history of Uganda, on the mineral wealth of Zaire or the financial crisis of some other country.

"You'll see. I'll bet you this stock is going to gain and that we'll sell it for twice the money on one month. We're going to be rich, sonny!"

Both of us break out laughing. We're both bums who prefer the stars in the night sky to those of the Palais Brongniard. And yet, a month later, Léon the Hobo is a virtual millionaire. His prediction was right on. Rather impressed, I ask him: "Why didn't you actually buy some stocks since they really did double and you were so sure of yourself?"

"With what money, my boy?"

"Couldn't you have found an old acquaintance or maybe a nephew willing make you a loan? Especially if you promised him interest?"

"I'm sure I could have, my boy, but the basic question is this: what would I have done with all that money?"

"You could have put it away, or reinvested it..."

"What for?"

"To buy yourself a house, some clothes... I don't know..."

"I had all that, young man. I had a house and a powerful car. I had everything a man could hope for. So what? It's all hot air, my young friend. It's a lot of hot air! It's all vanity! I'm much happier in my five star train car, dressed in my cashmere coat with built in ventilation. What do I need today? A little friendship... that's something money can't buy!"

I've got nothing to say to that. I'm all too aware that love isn't something you can pick up at the mall.

The evenings I spend with my friend are exquisite. He's an old original who has chosen to stand outside this ailing human society. He's given me a taste for history and geography, conveying his humility before his knowledge, he invites me to receive from every person the share of light they hold within them and always to keep a finger on the world's pulse, particularly that of Honduras.

Chapter 14

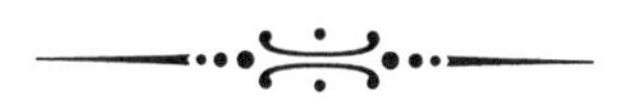

The Great Escape

Every evening, when Monsieur Léon and I go our separate ways, a kind of depression starts settling in around my chilling solitude. I feel as if I were leaving my grandfather. As if I were trading a trusted and affectionate friendship for a hostile world. In order to reach the Eiffel Tower and my bike hangar, I have to make my way through neighborhoods where the police make regular rounds. Their linear streets offer few places to hide. In spite of my job that provides some security, I'm constantly on the lookout.

One night, after accompanying Monsieur Léon back to his abandoned Hilton in the Auteuil train station, I get nabbed by the cops on Singer Street. No way out. They don't mean any harm, but haul me off all the same. As I'm getting out of their wagon at the station, I trip. The policeman accompanying me loses his balance; that's my cue, I'm off. I run like a madman all the way to my bike hangar. Too late, it's locked. I start heading toward Bir-Hakeim… Cops! The word must be out. I turn toward the military academy, then down the Invalides, I thread my way through University Street, turn onto Leroux, then onto Sèvre: more cops! What is this? A convention, a protest or just a night for being gung-ho?

I hide behind a hedge on Boucicat square, they pass by without seeing me. Next, direction Bonaparte Street. There, at the corner with Saint-Pères, I come face to face with two men who grab me by the arms. Plain-clothes cops, damn! They've got me.

"Do you have ID? What are you doing in the street so late? Your parents allow this? Where do they live?"

I keep my mouth shut. I'm in a tight spot, these guys are tough. More than anything, I'm worn out, I'm tired of running, I feel like I've been running for years, like I'm constantly afraid, I've had enough. A tremendous sense of weariness comes over me. I'm throwing in the towel.

They radio their colleagues and load me into their paddy wagon. I offer no resistance. The atmosphere is tense as we arrive at the police station. They put me in with the adults. I'm barely fifteen, I look more like eighteen. They pull me from the cell. I wind up between two cops: one's sitting in front of a typewriter; the other is standing, conducting the interrogation. Standard questions: "What's your name? Where do you live? What's your parents' name? Etc." I don't want to say anything.

The one doing the talking asks kindly: "Are you hungry?"

I nod. He brings me a sandwich and a soda. We eat together. I answer his questions.

"Guénard, Philippe, fifteen or sixteen, I'm not sure... Orphan, no, I mean abandoned... No address for my parents... Yes, I sleep in the street... Yes, I escaped from the correctional facility in D., it's been nearly three years...

I tell them my story, leaving out the illegal parts, of course. The cop's in seventh heaven, he's hanging on my every word, catering to me hand and foot. He can't get over it. He's never known a runaway to get by for so long without getting nabbed. His colleague's banging away like a madman on his old machine.

After my deposition they put me back in a cell for a few hours then haul me off to the Quai aux Fleurs. On arrival I get searched, a few things get confiscated and it's off to bed in a three-man cell with the head in a corner, just like in the movies.

The next day I'm led into a large room with a single, barred window, where about fifteen other people are waiting. I'm the youngest one there; that gets me going. I start showing off and bragging and accidentally bump into one of the guys. His reaction is abrupt:

"Hey, little runt, get out of here or I'll bust you one!"

He raises his hand to hit me, but another guy, a Slav built like a house, grabs him by the arm:

"Don't touch him, I recognize him, he's Jacquot's brother."

The guy who wanted to turn me into mincemeat is suddenly quiet, gentle as a lamb. My protector turns toward me: "Don't you recognize me?"

I'm thinking, trying to remember. No, I can't say that I do.

"I'm a buddy of Mario's son."

"Oh, right, I remember you. You used to help him out at the restaurant."

"What the hell are you doing here?"

"I got busted on Saint-Pères Street. What about you?"

"I rearranged the mug on some restaurant owner over by Saint-Sulpice. He pissed me off, I busted the place up and got in a tussle with the cops. They'll have my number, I was on parole..."

"What's a parole?"

"It's like monitored freedom. I'm sure you'll get out before I do... Remember, Mario likes you and hasn't forgotten you. The old guy's loyal to his friends!"

"Yeah, he's nice. I like him too."

"So, what's become of your brother, Jacquot?"

"He's on vacation."

"So you're by yourself?"

"Yeah, but that's nothing new. I'm used to it."

We get separated. I return to the cell I spent the night in together with a strange guy with an ugly mug. I tap on the pipes, the neighboring cells respond, it helps the time go by. I don't trust this other guy. Without a word he keeps his eyes on me, like a chimpanzee that's up to something.

Forty-eight hours later, the officers take me to the courthouse at the Quai aux Fleurs. The first time around it's impressive. From a humid jail with dark corridors, I find myself in a large and luxurious setting, like a banquet hall. We emerge from ancient underground structures onto enormous staircases with people running past one another in a muffled bustle. I get seated on a bench. A perfect place to observe the judicial hive at work. An officer orders me to follow him. I enter a room with ceilings tall enough to fit three stories.

A secretary is sitting in front of her typewriter. I sit down. A door at the far end opens. The officer salutes:

"Good day, your honor."

The judge looks me over. I examine him. It's only natural, he's my first judge. He opens a file lying in front of him and starts talking, occasionally flipping through papers, occasionally glancing at me over the rim of his glasses.

"So, young man, we've escaped from a correctional home?"

No answer.

"May we know why?"

Silence.

"Come on, why did you run away?" He's getting upset.

"I don't want to stay in a correctional home."

"And where would you like to go?"

"To my mother's."

Awkward moment. He's perplexed. I don't know why I said that. It's a stupid line that came out all by itself, an impossible wish. I said it and he's not answering. He clears his throat.

"Alright, I suppose you're going to be reasonable now. I see you've frequented some rather shady characters. Young man, I can only hope that your experience will have knocked a little sense into you. Once you're twenty-one, you'll do whatever you like. But for now, you're going back to the correctional home..."

"No, I don't want to!" I yell.

"Young man, you don't have a choice in the matter, and I'm not asking your opinion!"

"I'll just run away again, you'll see! You can't do this to me!"

Now I'm screaming and shaking like a leaf. I can see the director, the supervisors, the dogs, I can hear the threats and the everyday stupidity. Never again! It's as if I were being sentenced to hard labor. The judge isn't listening, he doesn't want to hear it.

I stare at him, defiant and angry. I'll see you again, little judge, and you'll regret it!

The officers handcuff me and haul me away. I'm off to Cayenne. A wagon takes us to the train station where I'm subjected to the shame of crossing the huge lobby between two officers with my hands tied. I feel so humiliated that if I could put a garbage bag over my head, I'd do so without hesitation. People are looking at me as if I were some kind of monster or a circus beast, with a mixture of fear and warped curiosity.

After two hours on a train, in a compartment emptied out just for the occasion, we arrive at the correctional home in B., in the North. My guardian angels turn me over in person to the director. He doesn't seem any more human than the one in La Rochelle.

Once the officers are gone, the bastard lays into me. Not by himself though, he's too much of a coward for that. A thrashing led three against one, the director and two supervisors. They say just how it's going to be:

"We're going to tame you!"

They hit hard, with fists, feet, elbows and knees. I fall to the floor. I refuse to let these bastards break me. I refuse to let this hell start again. My hatred is boiling over, it turns to fury and fills me with violence. With one step I'm up and, pouncing on one of the supervisors, I start wildly yanking his hair and screaming. I don't want to let go, I don't want to let go. I'm going to pull his hair out. My nerves are raw. A kick to the stomach knocks the air out of me. I collapse in pain. They stand me up and force me to walk, pulling me by the ear.

They stick me in building C. I get a warm welcome from my brothers. My reputation has preceded me. They dub me "the getaway king." An hour later I'm at the doc's office for shots and off to the barber to get my head shaved.

Then the supervisors in section C take me aside:

"If you don't toe the line, punk, we'll have you pegged. We've got orders to keep a tight lid on you."

I manage to keep myself from spitting in their faces. One of them walks behind me, grabs my ear and pulls hard. My nose starts to sting, a chill runs up my spine, everything turns red. I spin around faster than Bruce Lee and my foot connects with his shin. The smug poser lets go of my ear and grabs his leg. He wants to fight back. I stare him down and say: "You touch me, I'll beat the crap out of you one day... or one night."

He falls silent. His two partners just grumble and start backing away. Right then I blow a fuse and scream:

"I'm nothing but a bastard, a little shit for my parents and for you, fine! You want to break me? Well I don't give a shit about this life. You want to tighten the screws, tame me? You don't scare me anymore, nothing scares me. I couldn't care less about life. You want to kick my ass? You're a man, have at it, I've got nothing left to lose!"

I move toward them. They just stand there, dumbfounded, like idiots. I can see fear in their eyes. There's a long silence. The kind of silence you get on the edge of an abyss. A silence where the worst can happen, where everything can topple. Nothing.

Nothing happens. There's no final explosion.

They take me back to the cafeteria. My brothers leave me a choice seat in the middle of the table. They start catering to me, they're proud of me: "You've got balls, man!" I don't say a thing. I can't get over the whole turn of events, I don't know what to think. My dreams start running wild, my whole world just caved in. I laugh, I start playing the tough guy. Inside, I'm as lost as a puppy in the jungle.

At the next table, the three supervisors are holding council under their breath, throwing sideways glances in my direction. I just stare them down arrogantly. My eyes are stinging, somewhere between tears and anger, and my ear's on fire. A festering rage is simmering within me.

We get up from the table. One of the supervisors—the least stupid of the three—comes toward me. The room falls silent.

"Guénard, you're going to follow us. We've decided that you've got to learn to obey."

They take me out to the soccer field.

"Clean it up. Pick up all the paper and all the leaves. It's got to be impeccable, Guénard!"

They hand me some trash bags. The two German Shepherds are on my heels the whole time. I don't have much room to maneuver, these massive dogs are terrifying. Still, I have to try to think. The next morning, the supervisors take me back out to the field. It's littered with leaves and paper, even though I left it spotless last night. I get it: these bastards emptied the bags I filled up. They dumped everything I had picked up.

"Start again, you pain the ass! You'll keep doing this until you can obey!"

I look them in the eye and, without raising my voice, I say: "In three days, I'll be done."

At that moment I find myself swayed by an uncontrollable desire to leave, to go very far away. For that to happen I have to put together an escape plan. Through their cruelty, these dolts are unwittingly serving my purposes.

I start picking up papers and leaves again, both dogs at my heels. Whenever the supervisors leave me unattended, I discretely retrieve the food I went off with during dinner and hid in my underwear. The dogs appreciate the bonus.

The next day, the field is covered with junk again. Good. Time for another round. I feed the dogs. They lick my hand. I've tamed them. I talk to them while I'm picking up the leaves. We make our way once around the field. The very first night, I spotted a portion of the fence that had been pulled up. Every time I go by it I tap it with my foot to make the hole a little bigger.

By the third day it's large enough for me to slide through. That's my cue. The next morning, at five o'clock, I slip through the opening. I'm not alone. A boy named Alain is with me. Impressed by my adventures, he asked if he could escape with me. I said: "OK, meet me at 5 am at the stadium." He's right on time. I've got no reason to deny him the trip.

My friends the dogs are whimpering. They follow us a while then, either out of a sense of duty or just knowing where their food is, they turn around. They remind me of Rantanplan, the dog from the penitentiary, in the adventures of Lucky Luke, who accompanies the Daltons whenever they're escaping.

Half an hour later we're on a train bound for Paris. The alarm must have sounded by now. Alain's afraid, I can tell he's nervous. He's getting on my nerves. You'd think he'd react just the other way around. I say: "Alain, breathe deep, relax, look out the window. You're free, enjoy it! And don't start pissing me off!"

The train rolls into the Gare du Nord. There are no cops at the end of the platform. Alain manages to calm down. Me, I'm "free" again.

Chapter 15

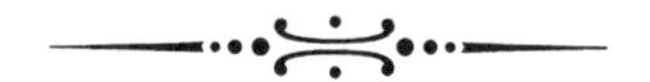

The Old Man and Death

I breathe deep to get a taste of the city's polluted air. Freedom! After escaping from the correctional home, just wandering aimlessly is a pleasure.

There's a cloud in my otherwise blue sky: Alain is starting to get on my nerves. He's nearly eighteen, I'm fifteen. He keeps whining. When I take him to my bike hangar near La Motte-Picquet, his expression turns to disdain.

"What? You call this a palace? You've got to be kidding. You think I'm going to sleep in this dump?"

He's cold, he's moaning and complaining. I can't talk any sense into him. Finally out of arguments and out of patience, I play my ace:

"Hold on, Alain. Tomorrow, I'll introduce you to some nice ladies. It's easy work and it pays well. You're eighteen, you could get yourself a hotel room."

No go! Mister Alain can't take it anymore, Mister Alain wants to go back to the correctional home. What an ass! We split up. Alain takes the train back to where he came from.

I'm realizing for the first time that I'm not like other kids. I'm fifteen going on sixteen, I like the streets, the freedom of the jungle, along with its risks, even if it is easy get lost there. Bike hangars to sleep in, bums to teach you things, rich ladies for a little tender loving that pays well and poor ladies to listen to you pour your heart out. I like the fancy apartments with silk sheets, the fear of cops that adds a little spice to the everyday, the snazzy threads, the pimps who'll pat you on the cheek with a kind word straight from a heart larger sometimes than you could ever imagine, and the monuments all over Paris. To me, this city is like water to a fish, even if I am pretty much alone in my fishbowl.

On Friday I run to La Coupole. I manage to set up a meeting with a lady I know. Two days later, my services rendered and my first paycheck in hand, I return to a restaurant around Montmartre where Jacquot and I used to eat. Just as I'd hoped, I find Freddy "the Fixer" and order a phony ID.

"No problem," he assures me. "You pay two hundred up front and the rest later. Follow me."

I give him the down payment and we hop a Metro to Place des Ternes. He asks me to wait for him by a large gate. After a couple of hours I'm realizing I've been had. This building's got two exits, Freddy used the other one. I start searching without any luck, swearing to make him pay for the theft and the insult.

One evening, about three months later, as I'm walking into a bistro down by République, I see Mister Freddy the Fixer hanging around the bar. I move up and start crowding him.

"So, Freddy, remember me? You didn't forget did you?"

He seems happy to see me. I don't buy all his talk or his list of excuses.

"Hey, Guénard, I've got your papers, they're at my house, I swear. Wait for me here, I'll go get them, I'll be back in an hour. In the meantime, you can drink to my health and on my tab, how's that?"

I let him think I'm playing along. An hour later, I show up at his little apartment with my buddy Jim, a friend of mine who's also on hard times. He comes to the door in his pajamas. This fool was getting ready for bed! We push him inside and my buddy unloads a right hook on him. He goes crashing into a table, spluttering. We swipe the dough and take off. We went easy on him.

In the meantime, I got my papers from my new friend Jim. He's from Bagnolet and he's a first-class schemer. We see each other often. He's not eighteen yet but he's totally on his own. His mother drinks, his father's in jail. Double absence. Whenever he goes home he finds his mother in a pathetic state. His heart aches for her: she sleeps during the day and gets drunk at night. When he tells me about her, his voice quivers, tears well up: he's a sensitive dreamer, he turns away to hide his tears. The shoulders on top of his tall lanky body shake with every sob and sniffle: "Come on, let's get out of here." We head out without knowing where we're going, we wander aimlessly. Jim's mother and my father are captives of the same poison. He feels pity, all I feel is hatred. In the evening we often go up to Auteuil to visit Monsieur Léon, our old friend. We bring him three slices of that ham he likes so much. We listen to him for hours, reconstructing a part of the world before leaving it hanging when dinner comes around. We bring the daily special, he unlocks the mysteries of the universe. With the modesty of a grandfather and the attention of a man who has suffered great losses, Monsieur Léon gives me an introduction to the secrets of sex.

"Making love is easy, it's quick. Then things get complicated. All too often, pain follows pleasure... My boy, think before you say 'I love you' to someone. Those words aren't meant to be said half-heartedly..."

Still daydreaming, Jim and I leave the tired old sage, both of us thinking of our own parents. Trying to forget our pain we start exploring the Paris night life in search of our daily dose of adrenaline. That drug's free. It's the only thing that quells my hatred. A little pilfering, a little vandalism...

One night at Auteuil, we're surprised to find Monsieur Léon's usual spot on the bench empty. We wait until eleven, no one. We go knock on the door of Léon's palace. Another vagrant, looking like a glum porcupine, is there instead. A bit worried, we ask him: "Hey, where's Monsieur Léon?"

The porcupine laughs: "Monsieur Léon's gone on the big trip!"

I look at Jim, I don't like the sound of this:

"That's impossible, he didn't say a thing. He wouldn't have left without a word. That's not like him!"

Porcupine takes a swig of red wine from a bottle, wipes his mouth and says: "Nothing to it. He couldn't have warned you, he didn't know about it either. Yesterday it was Nénesse, today, Léon. They've gone. . ."

Silence. Porcupine burps.

"...to the big Boss."

"Who's the big Boss?" I demand, shoving him.

Porcupine's starting to get on my nerves with his riddles.

"Hold on there, young fellow, hold on! The big Boss is the one who calls all the shots, the master of life and death. He's also known as the Eternal One. Léon, on the other hand, wasn't eternal. He died at ten o'clock this morning. He was hit by a car on the boulevard. Don't worry, he didn't suffer. He died instantly."

Utter shock. Monsieur Léon, dead...

Impossible.

We leave without a word. I can't go on without my adopted grandfather. My life as an unwanted adolescent doesn't begin to make sense without his presence. We don't care about Nénesse, we didn't know him. It's not like with Monsieur Léon; he can't die. I'm mad at the big Boss for taking my friend without asking. That evening the Eternal One gets a good talking to.

After bewailing our loss, we split up. Jim heads home to Bagnolet to find his drunk mother and more tears; I make my way back to my bike palace with a chilling sense of loneliness. My confidence is gone, something in me has shut down. It's like a landslide inside my heart, a crevasse that's sucking me in.

Everything I try to build collapses.

The days that follow are marked with sadness. Monsieur Léon's absence has left a tremendous void. That evening, Jim and I buy a copy of the *Times* in honor of our old friend. Finding a bench to sit on, we hold forth on various topics. Our heart's not in it. Neither is our level of culture. That puts a quick end to that little ceremony. Our world is crumbling, it hurts.

A few days later, Jim doesn't make it to our meeting place. I find out from the gang that he's in jail. He beat up some guy who was taking advantage of his drunken mother. He hit a bit too hard, the guy wound up in the hospital. So here I am, alone, feeling about as light as a funeral procession. What's the point of this hard-knock life? Why the constant upheaval? I have no idea. Big black hole. Granted, my friendships have given me more satisfaction than I ever got from my delinquent ways, but they're gone now. And yes, I'm mad at the big Boss who must be laughing from the height of His heaven.

Wallowing in my depression, I let my guard down, my vigilance starts flagging. The cops nab me a few days after Monsieur Léon's death. I let them take me. They haul me off to the station then to the judge. It's the same thing as last time. My only consolation is the sympathetic smile I get from the judge's secretary.

"Hey, you're back?"

"Yeah, I'm here to see the ol' penguin."

I didn't hear the penguin come in. He looks at me, scowling, hands on his hips:

"You again, young man? What do you want?"

"I already told you, I want out of the correctional home."

Silence. He sits me down.

"What am I going to do with you? Any ideas?"

I answer calmly:

"You have to kill me! That way I won't bother you anymore. I'm telling you, as long as you're two-faced, I'll keep coming back just to spite you."

The penguin doesn't seem too surprised, I guess he's heard worse. He lets out a sigh without smiling, picks up the phone and starts talking to who knows who with a worried look on his face. Evidently he doesn't want to kill me. That's something of a relief.

Chapter 16

An Open Letter to My Father, the President of France

A few minutes after a phone call placed by my somewhat perturbed judge, two police officers come and take me away. I fear the worst all the while hoping for the impossible: am I going back to the correctional home? Or is there another solution? The penguin didn't give me the slightest hint.

We cross Paris in a police van. It's dark out.

"Hey look," says one of the cops. "See the crowd over there in front of that house? Do you know who lives there? It's the singer, Claude François. He's always got girls at his front door."

These officers are nice guys. They're taking me to a new correctional home. I can't believe my eyes. There's a foosball table and Ping-Pong. This is prison deluxe.

The next day I find a typewriter on a table and think to myself: "Cool, I'll become a writer." I can't find the third letter of my name... wham! I send the whole contraption into the wall, smashing it to pieces.

There's a good atmosphere, the food is great, I like my wayward brothers. I start thinking it was actually pretty nice of the judge to send me here. It's too good to last. The third day, around noon, a plump little woman with her hair up in a greasy bun comes looking for me. She's from Social Services. I'm seriously collecting the ugly ones.

"You, grab your bag and follow me."

She speaks softly. I don't have a bag so we head straight out.

Where to? My goon isn't saying a word.

Our first stop is the Gare du Nord; bad memories. Oddly enough, I find myself missing the handcuffs and the two officers. This time around, I'm just a nobody. That's even more humiliating than being a famous and fearsome delinquent. I can't show off.

My bodyguard's not very talkative. After an hour-long train ride we get to where we're going. We walk to the courthouse, near the cathedral. I take a seat on a red, late-eighteenth-century bench in an endless corridor. I can hear the snickering of nasty memories. The assistant enters an adjacent room. I'm just imagining how many homeless people could be sheltered in this hall. An officer taps me on the shoulder drawing me out of my humanitarian entrepreneurial daydreams.

"Young man, the judge is waiting for you."

Judge? What judge? A diminutive woman is standing in the doorway, looking peppy, a bit tough, about as promising as the woman from Social Services.

"That would be me, young man. Follow me!"

I'm thinking: "Darn, I never should have asked for her as a judge. She looks like a dragon.

She came recommended by several of my brothers. They talked about her like they would a mother, all choked up. All I wanted was a mother, that's all I'd hoped for. I didn't really care that she was a judge. So I asked to be transferred. The judge in Paris was only too happy to pass a troublesome case on to his provincial colleague.

When the judge orders me into her office with her stern face, I comply sheepishly.

"Have a seat. Let's review your case, Mister Guénard."

She opens my file, starts reading. Long minutes tick by. As she makes her way through page after page I can see tears starting to form in her eyes, the way they would with Jim whenever he spoke of his mother. After a few minutes of silence, she raises her head, looks at me attentively and says:

"Young man, what do you want?"

I don't trust that line that they all spout so easily. They're the ones who decide our fate without ever taking anything we want into account. I tell her the same thing I told the last judge:

"I want out of the correctional home. I don't want to become like my forlorn brothers and sisters. I don't want to go stealing a pair of shoes, a pair of pants or a Moped then, once I'm twenty-one, get transferred from the little prison to the big one just to rot a part of my life away!"

"Young man, whether you like it or not, you're out of the correctional home. They don't want you back!"

Shock! It takes me a minute to let this inconceivable bit of news sink in. Suddenly, I'm up from my bench like a soccer player who just scored the qualifying goal. I want to hug my judge. I can feel my entire being uplifted by an incredible sense of joy. My dream came true: I got kicked out of a correctional home! That's never been done before! I broke my torturers!

"So, young man, what do you want?"

My judge... she's kind of funny. She just got through telling me I've fulfilled one of my greatest dreams—that I'll never again set foot in that underage prison—and she's already asking me how I envision the rest of my life. I've never even thought about it...

I make a quick run-through of possible jobs and answer her off the cuff, as if I had just drawn the lucky number:

"I want to be a cook in the Navy."

After a moment of reflection, she gently suggests:

"I don't think that's a job for you..."

"Why not?"

"You're too hot-headed. Communal life doesn't seem to be your thing. What else?"

I'm out of ideas. I've never tried to imagine my future.

"Anything! Give me a chance, you'll see, I'll come out on top!"

I'm ready for anything. My release from the correctional home, my victory over those sadistic bastard supervisors has got me flying high, totally confident. I want to live, I want to fight to win; I want to win to be a man; I want to be a man so that one day I can carry out my revenge against my father.

Killing my father... It's one of those dreams that keep me alive.

I'm in all this shit because of him. He's got to pay for everything he broke, for my broken legs, my broken nose, my busted eardrum, and all the love lost... That's something that no one with even the slightest bit of honor can forgive.

"So, young man?"

"Uh, sorry ma'am, my mind was wandering. I don't know... Whatever you want... Give me a chance, I'll make it!"

Madam my judge looks at me affectionately. I can see why my brothers talked about her with such feeling and respect. As if I were praying, I keep repeating:

"Give me a chance, just one chance! Trust me, I'll win out!"

I'm ready to take hold of any outstretched hand, and hers is a beautiful one that I have no desire to let go of. She looks out the window for a moment. She seems to be contemplating the cathedral. After a long silence she says:

"Son, how would you like to be a sculptor?"

I'm a bit hesitant, I have no idea what the word means.

"Skull... what?"

"See the cathedral there, out that window? And can you see the beasts that are carved into the stone around the gallery?"

"Yeah, sure, the laughing monsters, right?"

"That's right. They're called gargoyles. They're seven hundred years old. Sculptors from the Middle Ages carved those in stone. Do you think you'd enjoy sculpting animals like that? I saw in your file that you're a good artist."

I said yes. I'd also have said yes if she had suggested I become a butcher or a plumber.

My judge grabs her phone and dials a number:

"I've got a good kid here, he's highly motivated..."

Hold on, is that good, highly motivated kid supposed to be me? I don't believe my ears.

"...Do you think you could take him on as an apprentice?"

The person on the other end says yes. No problem, sounds good. The receiver still pressed against her ear, she gives me a wink. I start imagining myself as a sculptor from the Middle Ages. Then she mentions my age:

"Impossible. He's six months underage. Either we have to wait or request a dispensation..."

"Darn! That's disappointing! Alright, thanks, we'll look into it, I'll keep you posted."

She hangs up, clearly frustrated.

"We have to wait until you're sixteen. At that point you'll know whether you've been accepted. Six months too young, that's a shame... Otherwise we would have to request a dispensation. It's time consuming and there are no guarantees..."

"Ma'am, what's a dispensation?"

"An authorization, a special permission, if you like."

"And who can give that special permission?"

"The President. I don't know if you realize the problems involved..."

"No problem, ma'am. I'm his son."

"...?"

"Sure! I'm the President's son!"

She's eyeing me up trying to figure out whether I'm joking, making fun of her or just from another planet.

I continue as seriously as ever:

"I'm not kidding, I'm the son of the President..."

"Right, of course, you're the President's son, I should have guessed. The thing is, you see, they forgot to mention that in your file and it's taken me a little while to catch on..."

"No ma'am, I'm not kidding. Let me explain. I'm a dependant of the state, an orphan, a Social Services kid. The President is my father. On every national holiday, at the correctional home, we would sing the national anthem in front of a picture of President de Gaulle, and the supervisors would always remind us:

'Stand up straight, this is your father.' But his picture sure didn't make him look like the kind of dad you'd want to play around with!"

That's not something you forget easily.

One day two cops stopped me, asked for my papers, my father's name, my mother's name... the usual rigmarole. I tell them my father isn't allowed to see me and my mother abandoned me... One of the cops is nice, he's got a sense of humor; the other didn't. He says:

"You've got parents, just like everybody else. So what are their names?"

"You want to know my father's name? I know you're not going to believe me... I have three dads: General de Gaulle, Mister Poher and now, Mister Pompidou."

The nice cop laughed, the uptight one blew a fuse. On the summons he wrote: "insulting an officer in the course of fulfilling his duty." No, you don't forget that kind of thing.

I say to my judge: "I'm going to write to him. We'll try and ask for that dis... authorization."

When you're poor, boldness and a sense of humor go a long way to keep you on your feet. I borrow a sheet of paper from the judge and start writing very carefully to papa President: "I need an authorization. Thank you for sending it along. I look forward to hearing from you soon. Best regards." My penmanship isn't all that great, but at least it's legible, even with spelling errors. The judge looks it over smiling.

"Young man, you have a stunning sense of logic!" she says.

She looks up with her beautiful green eyes, like high beams, making me dizzy, sending me into hypnosis. She takes an envelope, slips my letter inside adding a note of her own and says:

"I'll make sure your request gets there, I promise."

Like my brothers and sisters, I too have fallen in love with this woman who knows how to listen with her heart.

A few weeks later, the President of France, Mister Georges Pompidou, my father, grants the dispensation I had requested. I'm nothing but a two-bit hooligan with a fifty-fifty chance of spending half of his life in jail. Mister Pompidou couldn't care less about a brat like me. He could have paid no attention whatsoever to those poorly written lines fraught with the errors of a lost child and worthless kid, since he gets piles of registered mail everyday, from all over the world and he's got an entire country to run and worries up to here. But no. This Mister Pompidou, in my own personal pantheon, has become a great man. Because he took the time to care for a little person without a voice. He made the effort to act on something seemingly insignificant, something for which he would never be recognized, that would never be published in the newspapers, nor be seen on TV, that wouldn't win him a single vote in the elections and wouldn't save France. For me, this unselfish act from the President and the judge's confidence—she who could very well have dropped my letter in the trash, claiming it had gotten lost in the shuffle of government services—are sources of humanity.

These people make me a better person.

Now that's a good judge. One who welcomes you and takes the time to look at the truth about you. It's precisely a judge that doesn't cast judgment. One who, having looked at you, will look at your file and work with you to find a way to rebuild your life. One who extends a helping hand, even if everything seems hopeless. I didn't think people like that existed. I've met too many judges and supervisors who just label you, get you down, pull the rug out from under you and destroy whatever foundation you've got left.

Very often, for a delinquent, the first people to show some human kindness are the cops, the judges or the supervisors. It's true that these are thankless jobs, but they're also crucial. A cop who kindly offers a sandwich and something to drink, who doesn't treat a suspect like dirt, is someone you remember. A real relationship can emerge during an interrogation. I've seen it happen. The enforcers can also be the ones to show a degree of caring.

Although it didn't seem like things were off to a particularly good start, the judge and the President make me want to fight to build my life. Most of all, they make me want to be like them. That's some pretty serious ambition for a street urchin to want to be like Georges Pompidou...

Then again, it's only natural... He's my father!

Chapter 17

Apprentice Gargoyle Sculptor

While we're waiting for my internship to start, my judge sends me to a technical school, in a transitional eighth grade. It works out well, I happen to be in transit...

The director gives me a compassionate welcome, as do the professors. The judge summed up my story for them. My French teacher, an attractive woman, divorced and frail, is especially considerate. I have huge gaps in learning, so she tutors me during recess. In the midst of my ocean of ignorance there emerge isles of knowledge. I even surprise my teachers with my eclectic knowledge of South American geography or of the French Revolution. Thank you, Léon. I hardly know how to write, but my classmates listen with admiration as I evoke a panorama of Honduras.

I come to the painful realization, once again, that I'm not like other kids. To my great surprise, I find they've never been out of the family cocoon or out of this area. From some of the teachers I hear: "That Guénard's too young to have gone through all of that, he's just laying it on."

And so my heart hardens and shuts off. I'm fed up with these dolts. As if anyone could be too young to have been beaten, abandoned, raped and corrupted! It seems the stupidity of mankind has reached Himalayan proportions. Their disbelief causes me the deepest pain because it's yet another way of rejecting me. Is living the unlivable supposed to be age-specific?

In spite of the hardship, these few months of waiting have been good for me. I like this school and my companions. My

French teacher has taken a liking to me. Her tender care extends beyond the tutoring she's given me free of charge. We discover more than simple grammatical agreement. A lost child tends to elicit a maternal instinct in a woman that can turn into love. And I'm so starved for affection...

Every once in a while I lose it and do something stupid, without going too far out of line. Things remain negotiable. I think of my judge. I don't want to disappoint her, I gave her my word. She keeps me on the straight-and-narrow. I'm practically disciplined. I get into a little harmless dealing, trading stacks of magazines for things like bayonets, silver coins of Napoleon III, brass lamps... With part of the profits from my trade I buy boxes of caramel candy in bulk and hand them out to my pals at school. I play the magnanimous lord. Still just showing off! It's just another way of buying affection.

It's easy to misjudge people. One guy from my class, named Jean-Luc, I listed a bit too easily in the "major ass" column. Big mistake! He quickly finds his place among the "very cool." Jean-Luc turns out to be a real gift for me. He's my exact opposite, he's not insecure and he's got a big heart. Plus he's got a good build and the girls think he's good looking. We have a good time together, flirting with the girls; we make a good team. On Saturday nights we go riding on his motorbike, taking a spin through the fairgrounds or at some dance hall. He calms me down whenever I feel like fighting. We eat and drink, all the while eyeing the girls. With him, time goes by very quickly.

All the best things come to an end. It's the bad ones that never seem to be over.

On September 15th, I start my apprenticeship to become a gargoyle sculptor. The first monster I come across is made of flesh and blood. It's the crew chief I have to introduce myself to upon arrival. He sizes me up, head to toe, a scornful look on his face, and says in a dry tone:

"Are you here to work?"

"Yes sir."

He continues his silent inspection, as if he were evaluating each of my muscles, weighing my bones. Before turning his back on me he says:

"You're the twenty-third person we've hired, you'll be the twenty-third to split before the end of the week."

What an ass!

He's already on my nerves, he's pissing me off, I feel like demolishing the guy.

In situations like this, I usually just wag my head from side to side. When I get a blank stare back from the guy, I take my cue, bury my knee in his family jewels and take off running. It's one of my favorite games, my version of "prison ball." The victim doubles over, gets his wind back, curses me out, calls me everything under the sun and sometimes comes running after me. I relish those intense moments, the chases, the suspense that adds a touch of spice to my life. I saddle my fear and bolt. I always win. So this boss is on my case for no reason? Hey, I'll make you dance, you bastard... I start wagging my head. At the buzzer, just as I'm about to nail him in the nuts, I remember my word: "Give me a chance, you'll see, I'll make it!"

I raise my head and stare at him as if to say: "You'll see." If I lower my gaze, if I let him shit on me, he'll crush me. So I hang on, staring him right in the eyes. And I notice a sign right above his head that says: "John XXIII Street." I don't know the guy. As a matter of fact, I didn't know that important people even had numbers, just like abandoned kids. Since I'm the twenty-third on the list who's going to split by the end of the week, I take a liking to this John 23 and adopt him as my buddy.

Being a sculptor in stone is a beautiful thing, it's noble, but before you can carve the stone you have to carry it. I strap on very heavy blocks and haul them up to the fifth floor of a tilting scaffold. My arms hurt, my legs hurt, my head hurts. I give myself a bit of verbal encouragement, saying: "John XXIII, buddy, you'll see, the twenty-third's going to be the winner." The workers start calling me "Joan of Arc," because I keep talking to myself. I let them talk.

If I keep muttering to John XXIII, it's because I've got no one to talk to about my state of mind, about being tired, about being discouraged. John XXIII ends up helping me so much that I finally get that damn boss to eat his words. I finish my first week. He can't believe it. The workers look at me with respect. I'm proud of myself.

As the weeks go by, I start stepping out on my buddy, John, number XXIII. My arms and my legs are building up, I'm getting strong. I don't need my mental whip anymore. The guys keep teasing, but it doesn't faze me. And since the apprentice gets to be the lackey, I make runs for the workers, picking up red wine, cheese, bread, newspapers, tickets to the races... I accept this discipline when it's kindly requested.

One day, as I bring him his order, one of the guys claims I shorted him on the change. Jack—that's his name—calls me a thief in front of everyone. Enraged, I start busting this clod's wine bottles. The boss comes running, carrying an axe handle. Jack redoubles his accusations: "He stiffed me!" At that point, I blow a fuse, grab the axe handle from the boss and start wailing on Jack. He's screaming and crying. The guys are trying to stop me. Impossible, I'm out of control. I get right up in Jack's face, threatening him. He puts his hand up to protect himself. He's begging me to stop hitting.

"I'll stop only if you tell the truth. Come on, tell the truth, you bastard!"

So the coward admits his lie in front of the boss and all the workers gathered there. Patrick, a young apprentice, says:

"You asked for it. Your plan hit a bit of a snag; that ought to teach you!"

Yeah, a snag with an axe handle... The boss calls me over. We get into his van and he starts in on me:

"Remember the Judge? Do you want to see her again?"

I remember the judge just fine, and my word. I say:

"What would you have done in my shoes?"

"I don't know... But whenever there's a problem, come see me after work and we'll talk it out. Don't go settling scores by yourself. Now get back to the others and don't go acting all cocky!"

This boss is a tough man, but he's straight up and fair, a real colleague. From now on, I'm off the hook. No more running errands, no more heating up the lunch plates.

Lunch plates... My heart aches at the slightest thing. Every worker brings his lunch in one of these things. I watch them unwrap their silverware, slowly and deliberately. Their care isn't intended for the things themselves but for the person that prepared them. The lunch plate is a sign of love. Tender care went into preparing this food, for the younger ones, by their mothers, for the older ones, by their wives. I don't have a lunch plate, no wife, no mother. This absence reveals my solitude. I'm an expert at making express camembert sandwiches. Whenever my colleagues are kind enough to share their plate with me, it's as if they were having me into their homes. When you're on the worksite, feeling cold and tired, a hot meal is comforting.

Sometimes I want them to think I don't live alone, that someone loves me and pampers me. I buy myself a can of baked beans with sausage at the local store, empty it into a lunch plate and tell them my girlfriend made it for me. I'm not so sure anyone's fooled... Jack tries to patch things up. One day we're working together on the same scaffold. He apologizes.

"You know, I was just trying to get your goat..."

"Well, congratulations, you got it!"

We laugh and share a glass of hot wine, the wind is freezing. Jack's also from Social Services; that gives us something in common. He's got two children that he loves all the more for having never known his own father. The only news he would ever get of him came when the government made a request that he contribute to the pension of this complete stranger... Jack works hard so he can buy a house. He saves every cent, which explains his stingy side. Eventually, I learn to admire and love him. After that experience, I swear to myself that I'll always try to get beyond any initial negative impression I might have of a person and see their heart. People are always worth so much more than the labels we give them.

My apprenticeship is rolling along smoothly. I've got my niche in the company and I like the work. It starts getting a little more complicated when I have to go to school, a few days a month. I have a class in industrial drawing that's way over my head because of all the geometry I never learned. To top things off, I managed to get on the teacher's bad side. One day, during one of his presentations, I told him he was way off the mark. He started arguing. That afternoon, in front of the whole class, I showed up with proof that he was wrong. That cocky bastard got offended and publicly humiliated. Only now I'm paying dearly for that bit of a social faux pas. Every time I bring him a drawing, he tears it up in front of the whole class.

For several months straight I put up with this treatment. Until this May morning when he destroyed my work yet again. I wanted that one, I worked hard on it. I can feel my temper rising, anger flowing through me like lava. I go back to my seat, taking deep, slow breaths, still holding my bits of paper. I set them down on my desk and calmly walk back toward his. I grab the folder where this teacher keeps his own drawings and look right at him as I start shredding them one by one, in front of the whole class.

"Now you know what it feels like," I say.

I walk out, slamming the door behind me.

The entire class takes my defense in front of the teacher. My classmates make the case that, sure, I'm a bit out of the ordinary, but there are extenuating circumstances: in spite of limitations, I work hard on my drawings and he's just being unfair. The teacher listens. Then he comes to find me in the hallway. We talk, one on one. I apologize. Then he apologizes. He pats me on the shoulder: "Come on, let's get back to the others."

During the following weeks he would ask me to participate more and start giving me free lessons in geometry and industrial design so I could catch up. I start working like crazy, I fight for him, so he'll be proud of me, and for the judge. I'm finally getting acceptable grades. But the biggest lesson I just got from this man wasn't in industrial drawing, it was in humility. He was able to piss on his own pride. He took a step toward me, for peace;

even though he had the upper hand, he's the one who had been offended. One heck of a lesson for a cocky kid.

I'm fitting in well at school and on the worksite. During the daytime, I live in a kind of harmony with myself. It's in the evening that the balance starts wavering, when the sun dips below the horizon. I begin sinking into sadness and rebellion. With the onset of night, my old demons rear their heads. My anguish mounts, it's off and running, especially when I'm passing lighted apartments or lively homes. Behind the curtains, I imagine the intimacy of this family, children playing with their parents or doing homework under their guidance. Through the open windows, I hear the clanging of dishes, laughter, quarrels, life. Within me is a beast seething with violence and jealousy: "Why them? Why are they so lucky? Why not me?" So I become a love terrorist, a tenderness vampire. The affection I'm not getting I make up for with blows. For the sake of revenge I dole out beatings to whomever has the misfortune of crossing my path. It frees me from my solitude. At least someone's looking at me, insulting me, running after me, taking an interest.

I keep getting hurt by people. The vulnerability of my gaping wounds is sustained by cruel injustice. They just seem to pile up. A child from Social Services is an easy prey for profiteers posing as benefactors. I noticed that with my guardian-torturer, and now with the legal guardian who's been looking after me since the beginning of my internship in sculpting. Every month I turn my five hundred francs of pay over to him. He puts the money in the bank. At least that's what he claims. After a year and a half of work I ask to have it so I can buy a Moped, since my bike's been stolen. Feigning innocence this bastard says: "But you don't have any money! Your account's empty!" He took my money and I've got no way to prove it!

For fifteen days I cover fourteen kilometers on foot in each direction just to get to work. Exhausted, fed up and disgusted, I end up stealing a police Moped in broad daylight, from right in front of the courthouse. I cover it with stickers and come right back to the police station the next day, straddling my loot. A cocky, angry kid trying to start something. Nobody stops me, the cops go by without so much as a glance.

So I keep the bike figuring it's a present from my father, the President, to make up for the injustice committed by my guardian.

Chapter 18

Age Sixteen
Dancing with Blows

One night as I'm out wandering with loneliness by my side, I see a large billboard hanging over a porch. On closer inspection I read: "Boxing Ring." A light bulb goes off in my head.

I can see myself, four years ago, in a Paris street. I've just been busted by the cops. Screaming mad, I swing a leg at the one pushing me into the paddy wagon. Later he questions me patiently, without any aggression or rancor, taking my statement down in a brown notepad. He offers me some candy saying: "With your build you could make a good cop some day, or a boxer."

Being a cop isn't the first thing a kid with my background dreams about. And yet the words of this generous man had sunk in. You never forget kindness, it gets written into your secret heart.

Boxer...

Out of curiosity, I make my way into the gym. Guys are pummeling sandbags in front of large mirrors. They're hitting, hitting hard, panting away amidst the smell of sweat. A tough guy comes up to me, about fifty years old. He's got the intense stare of someone you can't begin to fool.

"What do you want, kid?"

My eyes half shut, I say:

"I want to box like them."

He looks me over in silence, feeling me out.

"Have you got a health certificate?"

"No, what is it?"

"Go see a doc, any doc, and explain to him that you want to start boxing. Ask him for the papers you need."

The next day I come back with a certificate. The tough guy with the radar eyes welcomes me with a smile.

"Hey, you got your paper!"

I can't wait to start fighting, I feel like hitting something. He hands me a jump rope: "Go on, like the others!"

I try getting this string over my head then under my feet, spinning it at the same time. I kind of suck at it. I get my feet twisted up in the rope and nearly hit the deck. The whole room finds my ineptitude rather amusing. My pride takes a beating. I'm looking like a young bull, lost in the arena, looking for a place to bury his horns. I manage to stifle my humiliation. I stay in spite of the challenge.

I go to the gym nearly every night. It's a release from my solitude that lets me pour my rage out onto sandbags rather than onto innocent victims. After fifteen days I start training in the ring with a pretty well-built guy who's been fighting for a couple of years. I'm really hyper. He's got a mean look that just makes me want to pound him. We trade a few blows. The trainer screams:

"Your guard! Keep your guard up or you're going to eat one!"

And wham! I take one right on the nose. I'm seeing red. It's automatic. I lunge, raging, punching, hitting everywhere and taking hits from every side when suddenly, wham! I land a right, Christian hits the floor. I get seriously bawled out and suspended for a week.

"You didn't listen!" growls the trainer. "This isn't street fighting, so watch it or you'll be dealing with me."

It's true, I was fighting the way I used to in the correctional home, when we would box without knowing what we were doing, without gloves, any old which way, just to imitate our older brothers. The tough guy's right, I'm here to learn a noble art and not to whale away like a savage. This suspension's a real lesson. I can mull over my stupidity.

I broke Christian's jaw. Since we're both in the same middleweight class, at a moment's notice I get asked to replace him in an exhibition at Saint-Quentin, for the opening of a European championship. I couldn't be happier. I don't regret even a little bit having sent poor Christian to the mat.

At my guardian's place, I train on bags of fertilizer to harden my fists and muscles. The sodium nitrate burns my skin. The best way to relieve the sting is to hit even harder. I start crying out of pain and anger. I imagine these inert sacks to be my father. That thought is my secret weapon. It shores me up during fights whenever I need a turbo boost to get to the next level and send my opponent to the mat. I think of my father... Then I start hitting harder, always harder.

On the work site, I give my arms a workout with the stones I have to carry. Everything becomes part of my training. My whole life is focused on my boxing rage.

I'm given the honor of fighting often. One match follows another. The tough guy has spotted me and starts giving me his time and advice. With exceptional finesse, he channels my violence and moves it through an intensive technical training. I often win my fights by knockout. My opponents' blows get me going, they fill me with rage. Now I can focus that power into a controlled and devastating shot. I'm hitting harder and harder and more and more accurately.

I get a kick out of seeing the other guy start swaying under my blows then collapse.

One day, that guy on the floor will be my dad.

During an exhibition in a town in Belgium, one of the spectators spits in my face as I'm climbing into the ring. The upper-cut I let rip knocks him out cold. After the fight, I head back to the locker and wham! I get right hook in the ear. Screaming pain. Rage. I turn around, ready to fight back, and I see my trainer, fuming.

"Yeah, I'm the one who hit you. That'll teach you to disrespect the audience!"

"I wanted to defend myself: that twerp spit in my face."

"Shut up, I don't want to hear it. A real boxer saves his punches for the ring. He respects his audience, even if he has to accept any humiliation they might dish out. A boxer is a pacifist, civilized, not a brawler. Go take a shower!"

Henri, the medic, takes the bandages off my hands and gives me a friendly pat on the head:

"Forget about it, Tim. Don't worry. He used to be like you. He likes you, you know. You're a lot like he was when he was young."

"He's got a funny way of showing it!"

"If he didn't like you, he wouldn't bother to ream you out! Alright, go take a shower. At least you got your knock-out."

"Thanks Henri."

He's misty-eyed. The shower calms me down. On my way out of the steam room, the trainer tosses me a towel.

"We're going to go celebrate your victory over at Antoinette's. Your foot-work's improving. Don't forget, you've got two fists, kiddo, so use them. You only use your left 10% of the time. That's a waste. We're going to have to work on that. For now, let's get some chow!"

"Yes sir! Sorry about earlier."

"It's history. Hurry up, kiddo, Antoinette's going to be mad at us."

An hour later, Antoinette, a friend of the gym who owns a restaurant, was treating us to her famous mustard-sauce rabbit. Three platefuls later, a rather charming Antoinette bursts out laughing:

"Hey Tim, I can see I'd be better off having your picture around than taking you out to dinner!"

She brings me a big dessert plate that I polish off, licking my lips. They're all looking at me open-mouthed and Henri says:

"Where do you put it all?"

"Hey, I'm a man! I could go work out right now, I'm in top shape."

My trainer laughs:

"Right! You couldn't even do thirty pushups!"

"Want to bet...?"

I get out of my seat, stretch out on the floor and pull off sixty pushups! For the last ten I feel like I've got the Eiffel Tower sitting on my rear end. But I feel like I can carry my Giraffe for the sake of Antoinette's beautiful eyes. There's a lot of motivation in showing off!

Ever since that slap in the ear and Antoinette's rabbit, there's a kind of complicity between us. I find myself in a wonderful time of real, manly friendship at the club. Training is like playtime in my life of misery and solitude. Now I spend all my evenings and weekends at the gym, awaiting the next fight.

The fight... Saturday night fever. Warm-ups in the locker room, introductions over the loud speaker, walking out, down the long tunnel, the tension in the arena... People are crowding around me. I make my way through this dense mass toward the lighted square in the middle of the shadows. I lean and step through the ropes. Henri ties my gloves on, pats me on the shoulder. There I am, small, alone in a corner, my stomach in knots while the crowd is screaming and my opponent is eyeing me from across the ring. The sound of the bell launches us at one another...

For me, a street kid, boxing is an extraordinary gift. Men take care of me, look at me, watch me, they teach me this subtle art that many consider crude out of ignorance. Boxing is an education in tenderness, in attention and humility.

After the fight, the loser accepts the verdict and the winner lifts up the one he defeated. Both men raise their arms and embrace each other.

But boxing isn't enough to drain all of my violence. Certain comments, attitudes or even a look are enough to make the storm rage. When that happens, I find it hard to contain my anger.

I'm working with Pierrot, a young guy, around thirty-five, a father to thirteen kids. He also went through Social Services. He drinks a lot. He's an alcoholic and spends more time lying down than standing. When he can get up, he's always looking for a fight. One really cold day, on a scaffold, he asks me for a tool and calls me a "son of a bitch." My blood boils. I throw my "pig's ear," my trowel, in his face. I sliced up his mug for insulting my mother. He whines and goes on sick leave for real. My boss sends me packing for three days. Pierrot won't ever be on my crew again. Just because she abandoned me doesn't mean you can talk trash about my mother.

After two years of internship, I earn my license as a sculptor. I'm not even eighteen. I'm the youngest recipient in France thanks to the President's dispensation. This day is a day of utter joy. I carefully fold my certificate, hop on my bike and tear up the sixty kilometers to the courthouse. I enter the huge building as if it were my home, find my hallway, my red bench and the door to the office of my favorite judge. I want to go inside. An officer says I can't because I haven't got an appointment. So I start screaming like a madman, calling up and down the hall:

"Madam Judge, Madam Judge!"

People start wondering what's going on, the cops want to throw me out, I keep screaming. Suddenly, my judge shows up. Whew, she heard me:

"What's going on out here? Oh, it's you? What are you doing here, young man? And why all the racket?"

"I kept my word, ma'am. I promised you that if you gave me a chance, I would win. I did it, I won! I got my sculptor's certificate three hours ago and I ran here to show it to you!"

I really think she can't quite believe it.

"Please, come into my office, young man."

I walk into the room and pull the precious document out of my inner pocket. I unfold it carefully, as if it were covered with gold dust. I hand it to her:

"Here, it's for you! I told you I would win."

"No, it's yours."

"No ma'am, I won it thanks to you. I won it for you and it's yours."

She senses my resolve. She takes my diploma and looks it over attentively. She whispers "Thank you." In her eyes, I see other words of thanks. I'm as happy as a king. I've just made the most beautiful gift of my life. Two years of perseverance, of fighting my demons, fighting cold and heat, fighting mockery and humiliation, fatigue and despair. It's a sweeter victory than any I've had in the ring.

I kiss my judge to thank her—she's still holding my diploma—and I leave her with a song in my heart. On my way by I call to the officer and the secretary:

"You see, I don't need an appointment! I'm her son!"

I head back on my bike to see my buddies, Jean-Luc, Jacques and the others. We toast my victory with a fantastic party.

At a police checkpoint a few days later, I come across the same oddball pair, the brigade's own Laurel and Hardy, the nice one and the idiot. I just bought a brand new, shiny motorbike to celebrate my success. The sly guy starts circling, looking for a glitch. Obviously, he thinks I swiped it.

"That's odd, I don't see a number on the engine..."

He circles, inspects, sniffs... I get so aggravated with his story of engine numbers that I walk over to their car that's sitting on the side of the road and, as if I suspected something, I ask:

"Is this your vehicle, gentlemen?"

I pop the hood.

"Are you quite sure this is the original engine? I can't seem to find a number on the engine... Strange... This car wouldn't be stolen by any chance, would it?"

Laurel's wearing a bit of a smile, as usual, whereas Hardy, who's got about as much of a sense of humor as I have patience, starts getting all uptight. He blows his top and screams:

"Don't go thinking that just because you're the judge's son you can get away with anything you want..."

He pulls out his pad and starts writing me up again for insulting a police officer in the performance of his duty—his specialty—plus a few extra bits.

"Believe me, I'll make sure this gets to your mother. She'll find out! And you won't get out of it that easily!"

I laugh and take off to see my judge:

"Ma'am, I'm here to let you know that I'm not only the President's son but your child as well, and that very soon someone will be bringing you a stiff fine. Don't worry about me though, I'm doing well and keeping out of trouble!"

I'm the youngest licensee in my union, but I'm also at the top of my class. Right away I start getting job offers. One of the inspectors is the boss at a large construction company. He hires me on the spot, skilled labor, level two. The law states that I have to present my diploma to my employer. Darn! I head back to see my favorite judge, without an appointment. The officer on duty lets me in:

"Oh, it's you again! Your mother's in her office."

Awkward moment:

"Ma'am, I'm really sorry, I completely forgot about this little detail: I need my diploma to get hired."

There it is in frame on display on her desk.

"Here you go, you deserve it, I'm proud of you."

"Thank you, ma'am, I'll bring you back the frame..."

"No, no, I picked it out with you in mind."

I'm all giddy inside, bowled over by her compliment. I leave her even happier than I was the last time. I'm proud that she's proud of me.

The next day I present my diploma in its golden frame to the company secretary.

"It's a work of art!" she exclaims.

I start strutting like a peacock. My boss quickly moves me up to level three and a few months later makes me crew chief. I've got a loud mouth, I'm competent and the men appreciate me.

I'm heading up a team of Algerians, Moroccans and Tunisians that I live with in a small worksite cabin. We're together twenty-four hours a day. I'll never forget my first night with them. The cabin's four meters long by two and a half wide. Across from the front door there's a sink beneath a window. To the left and to the right are bunk-beds against walls covered with posters of naked women in any number of positions. There's the nauseating smell of sweat and urine lingering in a stuffy atmosphere.

My first night, I didn't sleep a wink. An Italian worker whispers in my ear: "Watch out! They'll try to goose you in your sleep." At the slightest sound I'm wide awake. At daybreak I'm safe and sound, exhausted. My four bunk mates are out cold.

They would become real friends and even brothers at heart, to whom I would owe a great deal. We wouldn't have chosen each other. Life did that for us. In the evening we eat in a neighboring bungalow where are food is prepared. Their families are far away, as is mine. They welcome me as one of their own. After the meal, the Tunisians play music, the Moroccans dance. Magic moments when these men, who've worked hard all day long, wearing their hands against cement and stone, begin drawing graceful melodies and delicate harmonies from their instruments. Our cabin becomes a lighted parlor from the *Thousand and One Nights*.

These men live on very little. They sacrifice themselves, sending the better part of their paycheck to their families. They finally get to see them one month out of the year. Then they come back for a long year of solitude.

One evening I find Mohamed in the cabin, on his knees in front of the sink. He's speaking, moaning, mumbling something unintelligible and lying on the floor. I tap him on the shoulder:

"Mohamed, are you alright?"

He doesn't answer and continues his lamentation. An hour later, during dinner, I ask: "Feeling better?" He tells me not to worry: that's the way Muslims pray. And I thought he was sick! Mohamed explains his faith to me along with its daily rites. I don't know a thing about Islam, nor for that matter about Christianity.

Our communal life lasts a year and a few months. When I leave to go boxing, these friends of mine sense my passion and my youthful energy. They encourage me, they're happy for me. When I go fight in a foreign country, I bring them back presents and souvenirs. Their gratitude touches me deeply.

I like dancing with blows. In the ring I find the footwork I inherited from Iroquois warrior ancestors, the quick strike, a certain grace in my movements, silent, disconcerting.

These weapons that my father left me, I spend my time working and sharpening them, to turn them against him.

I love boxing. I've got it in me, it's perfect for me. Finally, I exist for someone. I get noticed. I get taken care of. When my eyebrow splits open, delicate fingers bring me a healing touch. They sit me down, they talk to me, take care of me, wrap my wounds, massage me, give me advice, whispering in my ear: "Go for it kiddo, take him from the right side, hang in there!"

For my victory, I get a congratulatory pat on the head and, as I climb the podium on the shoulders of my mentors, the crowd cheers. For me, the child without a name. They all want to be my friend.

I won't forget that I had to step into the ring to gain that acceptance. I won my share of tenderness by the strength of my fists.

The night of my first victory at the nationals, to celebrate the occasion, I feel the need for a setting worthy of my happiness and my pride. I manage to get away from my trainers and my small group of fans. I start walking through Paris that, without a doubt, is lit up just for me. Slowly, savoring my title, I cross the streets I had once wandered with solitude at my heels. I treat myself to a royal suite in one of the biggest hotels I had dreamed of. Worried that they might not let me in because of my age, I pull out the whole wad of bills from my victory and set it on the counter. I pay in full.

"Have you got any luggage sir?"

"No, no luggage. Just my gloves, and I'll keep those with me..."

In the elevator, a sharp-looking bellhop eyes the pair of fists hanging around my neck. He looks me over, notices the stitches in my face, the taped eyebrow, the bruises, the signs of a fight.

He doesn't ask any questions, shows me into the large suite and closes the door, leaving me alone with the high of my victory.

I set my gloves down on the royal sideboard and lie down on the enormous bed with its silk sheets. Far, far away from my bike hangar.

For the first time, being alone doesn't feel like a burden. It feels as light as champagne bubbles.

Tonight, I'm the winner. I'm stronger than my father.

The next day, I wouldn't leave my suite until noon. On the dot! So as not to miss a moment of this great comfort that I earned with sweat, blood, fists and hatred.

Chapter 19

Age Eighteen
Discovering the Aliens

Jean-Marie is a funny kind of guy. We're taking a training course in masonry together, in Compiègne. He's got frizzy hair going every old which way, a puny frame—you'd think he was made out of matchsticks—and always wears this blue and white striped sailor's tee-shirt. You'd think he was born with it. On the beach at Merlimont, he knits sweaters for his friends while reviewing his notes on reinforced concrete. But more than anything, his eyes light up when he talks about God—he talks about him a lot, it's kind of a hobby—sort of as if he'd just smoked a joint.

Honestly, I wonder what the hell he's doing in construction, looking like a lit-up, mystic artist type.

One day, in the courtyard, a small group starts forming around him. Jean-Marie starts talking about God again with his passionate testimony. Everyone is under his spell. He's getting on my nerves, swiping the spotlight like that, especially with that topic. I go up to him and say:

"You claim that God came into the world for the sake of the poor?"

"Yes, I do…" he says with that glow in his eyes.

"For all the poor?"

"Yes, of course, for all the poor…"

"Where was your God yesterday?"

". . ."

"Did you read the paper?"

". . ."

"The lady that got stabbed fourteen times? The child that was raped and beaten? Where was your God of the poor while that was going on? Off on some island?"

Silence. I'm relishing the effect of my stone in his pond. I'm thinking I shut him up for good. Well, no. He starts up again. He doesn't back down, he keeps talking passionately about his faith. He claims that every person is the object of God's boundless love, that that's the Good News and that his job, as a Christian, is to spread that message of love.

He also assures us that God weeps with those who are weeping and that his Christ on the cross took all our suffering on himself, every betrayal of mankind, in an act of boundless love. His resurrection is a promise of eternal joy. Etc. All that and more incomprehensible ideas.

Jean-Marie talks from his gut. You really feel something when he's talking. I find him annoying and challenging all at the same time. This Christian's got enough courage not to bail on his God when the going gets tough. He doesn't jump out of the arena when the lions of contradiction are let loose. He doesn't spit on his commitment.

This boy's not like the others. I find him intriguing. I get the sense of an inner drive in him, a joy of some kind, a profound peace I somehow find compelling.

So far I've left God out of my address book. On more than one occasion, when I really had it bad, I called on the unknown God, the almighty savior… No one came down from heaven. A beaten and abandoned child, a sick person, agonizing in solitude, a woman in labor, a man whose life is in the balance after an accident, all of them cry out for help from a Supreme Being, even if they don't call him God.

I cried for help. No one answered. I listed God as missing in action.

I find Jean-Marie appealing and disturbing at the same time. I like provoking him, backing him against a wall. For example, one day he came and knocked on my door. I take the knife I was just training with and chuck it at him, burying in the wood right next to his hand. I laugh. Him... not so much. He's a bit out of sorts. I'm all proud. He doesn't get discouraged. He comes back to see me the next day. This guy's impressive!

He surprises me also because he doesn't act like everyone else. During one recess, as I'm trying to get his goat by taking pot shots at the neighbor's cat, he asks to borrow the rifle for a minute. This guy comes out of his house, fuming, sees him with the weapon in his hand and, figuring he's the one responsible, starts reaming him out. Jean-Marie takes it all without a word of protest, without claiming his innocence. Not only does he take the fall, but he apologizes to the irate neighbor. I feel kind of bad for having let him take the blame, but he doesn't hold it against me.

One Monday morning I ask him what he's been up to all weekend.

"I went on a pilgrimage to Chartres," he says. "There were forty-five hundred of us. We walked, prayed, played music, it was fantastic!"

"Really? What do you do that shit for?"

"...In fact, I prayed for you, Tim, and for young people throughout the world."

"Really? I didn't ask for anything. Thanks anyway. So how many slugfests were there at this thing?"

"Slugfests? What's a slugfest?

"Scrapes; you know, fights..."

"Zero, no slugfests, no fights."

I can't believe it. I make him tell me again. I know he's got to be totally full of it.

"No fights? Do you swear on your mother's life?"

"No fights, and I don't have to swear for it to be true."

I watch his mouth, I read his eyes, he's not lying. It's unbelievable, impossible that there weren't any fights. I went to the county fair in Compiègne this past weekend. There were fifteen hundred people and I got into seven fights. And that's not counting a boxing demonstration on Saturday night. With music blaring in your ears and alcohol heating up your veins, there's always someone there to light my fuse and get things rolling. For me, where there's a crowd there's an argument, a provocation and a fight. Bing, bang, boom, it all happens pretty quickly, sort of like love. You meet, there's friction. If the guy's cool, he could become a buddy. If he's an idiot, forget it! Those are all memories of solitude. They fill your brain when you've got nothing else to put there.

Jean-Marie breaks in on my thoughts: "Why are you staring at me? I'm not from Mars, you know!"

"Yeah, you are! Forty-five hundred people and no one thrown down, you guys are whack! You could have been in twenty fights each!"

"No fights, you've got my word!"

Over the rest of the week I mull his story over from every angle. Pilgrimage, no fights. Apparently I haven't seen everything.

I ask him again about the event. He tells me he accompanied some handicapped people. That's right, he lives with handicapped people.

Wait a second... this guy's trying to tell me, with a totally straight face, that he works for loonies for free, and on top of it he spends his weekends with them!

I grill him; I want to know more about this alien.

Jean-Marie lives in a home that's part of l'Arche, in Compiègne, with about ten mentally retarded people. L'Arche, he tells me, was founded by an ex–naval officer turned professor of philosophy, a Canadian named Jean Vanier. This great man, disgusted with the way society rejects certain mentally retarded people and treats them like vegetables in psychiatric wards, pulled two of them from an asylum. Their names are Raphael and Philip.

When Raphael was a child, he developed meningitis. He can't speak anymore; his body leans, always off balance; you could say he's a few cards shy of a deck. It's the same with Philip. When their parents died, they were put in this hospital, behind high walls, as if they were lepers. Jean Vanier came to get them. With his two new friends he settled into a little house in a village called Trosly-Breuil, about twenty kilometers from Compiègne. The old traveler with a heart of gold found out how much Raphael and

Philip had suffered from being rejected by those around them and by society as a whole, as well as from the disappointment they had unwillingly caused among their relatives. He realized just how much they were in need of friendship and trusting relationships. He started listening…

Jean Vanier's idea really hit home and started gathering momentum. Since 1964, throughout France and in a number of other countries, mentally handicapped people live together in communities, with helpers who share their lives.

"It's not always easy," says Jean-Marie in his passionate way. "Living in community life transforms us. It lets us get at the heart of things. We come to help those in need and quickly discover that they're the ones who help us…"

"What's the heart of things?"

"Through l'Arche, we learn that we were made to love. We try to put all our abilities to work building a more loving society, where each person has a place."

"A loving society? You're kidding, right?"

"No, Tim. L'Arche is a sign that human beings aren't condemned to slugfests, as you say. Nor to war, nor to fighting where the strong always crush the weak. Love is possible! Every human person is precious and sacred…"

I listen in amazement, dumbfounded. This guy's totally high! He's talking about a world beyond my own, one I can't begin to understand, but fascinating nonetheless. Secretly, I find more truth in his world than in mine. I've got nothing but show and violence. I've raked in several boxing and wrestling titles. People crowd around me, flatter me, surround me. Coffee, restaurants, night clubs, I get it all for free. My reputation has swollen the ranks of my gang that's now got about fifty kids in it. They get to bask in my glory. We scour the area in a sixty kilometer radius. I'm a big chief. My second dream has come true.

But I'm unhappy. I don't know why.

My life is too hectic for pondering great philosophical questions.

One day, while I'm talking with some friends in the street, a really nice car pulls up next to me. A distinguished looking gentleman comes toward me. His chauffeur is standing outside, holding the door open. One of my buddies whispers in my ear:

"Hey, check out the bigwig heading your way!"

Kléber's right. This guy, dressed to the hilt, is really coming over to me. He greets me: "Good day, sir..."

Okay, that's weird. That's the first time anyone's ever called me "sir." He congratulates me on my record and adds:

"My wife and I would be greatly honored to have you to dinner next Thursday."

"Alright, why not? You can't turn down a good meal, right? By the way, who are you?"

"The chief of police, sir."

He waves and gets back in his limousine. I'm utterly dumbfounded. Before becoming a little champ, I was a bad kid. Now the police chief calls me "sir" and invites me over for dinner. My buddies start giving me flack:

"So, just like that, Mister Tim's headed off into the great big world?"

I let them talk.

The following Thursday, I arrive at the address I was given. A servant opens the door and takes my leather jacket. A funny look comes over his face as he notices the back displaying an eagle with a skull in its beak: my gang's emblem. Alfred regains his composure and shows me in. As I enter a large living room I find a number of people all huddled together. Everyone turns to greet me. I'm introduced to the mayor, the police chief, a senator, an industrial contractor and a banker. They're all in fancy clothes, dressed to the nines. I'm the only one without a tie, in jeans, wearing a collarless shirt, a bandana around my neck, my biker boots with six straps on each side and a riveted leather wrist band (comes in handy in a fight).

Mrs. chief of police sits me down just to her right—my kind of woman. I've never seen so many utensils on one table, you'd think they'd emptied the cupboards! I've got three plates, two knives, two forks and two spoons in front of me. All silver. I sit through dinner admiring my table paraphernalia, trying to guess which one to use. Well, that and eyeing the police chief's wife: fine! The others, the "suits," are getting on my nerves. It's almost indecent how they're buttering me up. The contractor thinks I'm great, the banker calls me "super." I'm thinking: "What do they want with me, and what does this guy think I am, gasoline or something?"

When I tell my buddies about the dinner their eyes grow as big as the double doors in the police chief's living room. They can't stop laughing. It's nice to let loose a bit after all that stuffy small talk. My real friends say:

"Come on, Milord. Now that you've hit the big time, let's go have ourselves a party!"

Showing off is my drug of choice. It helps me handle the insecurity I feel from being so different. My life is a whirlwind, it's all an act. Inside, behind the healthy, rugged façade, my heart is sad. My existence is about as dull as a carnival without any fights. The highs from boxing and all the compliments just don't cut it.

Now Jean-Marie, there's an authentic guy. He's not playing around. He says what he believes, he lives what he says. I find that oddly disturbing.

One Friday I catch up to him in the locker room where we're doing our internship. We change out of our work clothes. I ask him:

"Will you take me to your get-together in Chartres this weekend?"

He tells me it's an annual pilgrimage and that we'll have to wait a year. I lose it:

"I figured your story was a crock! You were leading me on and now you're backing out!"

Furious and disappointed I pop him right in the head and slam the door behind me on my way out of the locker room. In the courtyard, the bell signals the end of classes. I take off, fuming.

I spend Saturday and Sunday the same old way, between crowds and solitude, between quiet forests and noisy fairs, between dance clubs and cafés. These two worlds impose themselves upon me and oppose one another within me. I feel as if my very survival depended on this physical contact with nature, on these long walks through the woods where I sometimes come across the gentle, innocent gaze of a deer, where I listen to the melodies of streams. Silently, I slip between the trees, make my way through the bushes, sometimes coming close enough to touch a doe or a stag. After a few hours spent relishing this natural environment, I get back to my gang for our usual Saturday night craziness. Amidst wild dancing and blaring sound systems, there's plenty of booze to go around, spins on motorbikes and rhythmic fighting as the girls look on. When the happiness of others comes and slaps me in the face, only excess helps me stifle the waves of my past that rise in me with such violence.

The following Monday, my friends from the program openly criticize me for going at it so hard with Jean-Marie. They tell me I ought to go apologize. I sneer back:

"Yeah, like that'll happen!"

I've got my pride and I'm holding what he said against him:

"Everything he told me from the beginning, he was just bluffing." Actually, I'm not so sure...

That same evening I decide to go and find out if he really lives with handicapped people. I pull up and leave my bike in front of the place, a small house in a little side street of Compiègne. I hear laughter and shouts of joy. I knock on the door. A handicapped girl opens the door and asks:

"Who are you? What's your name?"

Struck by her condition, I remain silent. She asks me three times. I'm speechless, me, the boxing champ, the tough guy. Jean-Marie shows up and says:

"This is my friend Tim. He's a great guy, you'll see."

I'm thinking to myself:

"This guy's really nuts. I smack him around and he claims I'm his friend and that I'm a great guy."

Jean-Marie leads me inside. I'm really not comfortable. Everything's a little beyond me, I've got no control over the situation. A handicapped boy comes down the stairs and asks my name. I tell him. He puts his hand on my heart and says:

"Tim, you're nice!"

Poof! His words are like the softest touch, like a knockout punch, but all soft and gentle. "Nice" isn't a name I've ever been given. Since the day I was born I'd only ever been a bastard, a little shit; now that I'm a champ, I'm suddenly super and awesome. This handicapped kid with his little pipsqueak voice and his misshapen mouth gives me this gift of a word and knocks me out cold.

That's right. The first time in my career I've ever been knocked out and I'm laid out by a handicapped kid.

For the first time in my life, within my heart, I've been brought to my knees.

"My name's Philip," he stammers.

He takes my arm:

"Are you coming to eat with us?"

I can't bring myself to say no. I follow his lead to the table. The meal is simple and joyous. They help one another. I'll never forget the menu: stuffed tomatoes.

I'm thinking as I watch them. This handicapped boy invited me in because I seemed nice, not because I'm a champ. He doesn't know anything about my titles, my CV, my hard times or my failures.

These people from l'Arche are aliens. They're not like other people. They have simple and direct relationships: they like you, they tell you; they don't like you, they leave you alone. They're all so spontaneously giving, and in a world that's so calculating. There's no showing off, no putting on a show... It's refreshing.

I remember Jean-Marie's strange words:

"L'Arche is a big family. It was brought about by the Holy Spirit to let our age know that the heart of man isn't to be found in knowledge, in intelligence, in technology or in power but in love. For that purpose, God chose to manifest himself through people who are suffering, the weak, the poor, the simple..."

I'm beginning to understand.

After the meal, everyone gets busy doing the dishes and telling jokes. Philip, my new buddy, asks me:

"Are you coming to see Jesus with us?"

Why not? I feel good around these folks. Suddenly I realize that to go see Jesus—must be one of their friends, probably Portuguese, with a name like that—I have to cross town with them. Hold on! You mean me, the Boxer, the big chief at the head of a mighty gang, with an eagle and a skull on my back, you think I'm going to wander through town with the same bunch of mentally handicapped people I was calling "retards" not two hours ago? Are you nuts?

No time to weasel out of it. Jacqueline, who opened the door for me, grabs me under one arm while another girl, Sophie, takes my other arm. And off we go, arm in arm, stumbling along. Jacqueline limps along, holding onto me. Sophie meanwhile, two inches from my face, keeps spluttering: "I like you, Tim, I like you." Behind me, the hall of wonders is out and about. I hope we don't run into any of my buddies; this would be totally embarrassing!

A half hour later, after having walk all the way across town, we finally arrive at our destination in a square in front of a church. A British guy welcomes us, saying to each person: "Greetings my brother, greetings little sister." I'm thinking: "Man, that's one big family!" He turns to me and says: "How are you, my brother?"

Wait a second! I don't know this guy, I'm not his brother! I've got brothers and sisters but we were separated. No way do I want to hear from a stranger a word that my family can't even give me. I'm going to smack this Brit. "Fellow citizens, strike first!" That's what Monsieur Léon used to say. Just about then, my buddy Philip tugs on my sleeve:

"Come on, we're going to go see Jesus."

Well, he got there just in time. I'm finally going to meet this famous pal, Jesus. I wonder if that could be the church caretaker.

We enter the chapel. Complete silence. I can make out a hundred or so people kneeling in the half-darkness. I stop, dumbfounded. Straight ahead, there's a spotlight shining on a large cross. Hanging on the crucifix, I recognize the guy I've passed by so many times along roadways, on roadside crosses out in the country, the highway robber with the long hair, half naked, a pained expression, a hole in his chest and nails in his hands and feet.

I goofed. Jesus isn't a Portuguese buddy, he's the one known as Christ.

Another surprise. The people aren't facing Jesus' crucifix, in the middle, they're all turned toward the left. What's with them, I wonder? In a whisper I say to Philip:

"Are they dumb or what? They're all looking over to the left and Jesus is over there. What's with that?"

Behind us I hear shushing. That's annoying. As he whispers in my ear, Philip points out an object in the shape of a golden sun sitting on a white table:

"That's Jesus; it's Jesus' body, the Blessed Sacrament."

If he weren't an invalid, I mean if he were normal, I'd be saying: "Cut it out, you're pulling my leg, what the heck are you talking about?" But he's so nice and patient with me I'd just as soon keep quiet.

I'm bored. I start looking around, watching. Some of the folks from l'Arche are on their knees, like my Muslim friends when they're praying on the worksite. Others are crouched down, eyes closed. Weird.

I look at the golden sun. I'm having a little trouble believing that people come from miles around just to stand in silence in front of a white, round something or other they call Jesus. Imagine a nightclub without music, without drinks and where no one budges! I know what hosts are. When I was a kid I ate hundreds of them out of the church tabernacle, where my guardian-torturer used to go. It's just bread. Plus I don't get any of their gibberish, Blessed Sacrament, monstrance and all that hoopla. It's all Greek to me. Or Latin.

What I find impressive are the expressions on people's faces. Some give off a luminous glow. They're all peaceful, calm, quiet. I say to myself:

"If they can see Jesus in there, there's no reason I can't. I'm not any dumber than the next guy. I'll give it a try. I'll get into the right position, and voilà! It ought to work."

I kneel for five minutes, I still don't see anything. I must have missed something in the instruction manual. Oh, right, eyes closed. It must be that you're supposed to start by closing your eyes... Let's try it out. I close them... Five seconds, ten seconds, fifteen seconds... Nothing, still nothing. I'm not going to spend the night in the dark! I open my eyes. Everything's right where it was before. And there's the little white host inside the sun that's still watching me...

I'm starting to get cramps in my legs, I feel like moving around. Just then, a guy in a long white robe gets up, goes and picks up the sun and takes Jesus behind a pillar.

"Hey, wait up, I didn't have time to see him!" I exclaim.

Seriously, a little warning wouldn't hurt! The guy in white turns around looking at me, the hundred people there turn toward me and it seems like even Christ on his cross is looking at me. They all have the same kind, amused expression on their faces. They must be thinking: "There's one who's a little more handicapped than the rest of them!" The guy in the robe puts Jesus away in a safe and locks him in.

That's strange, why's he doing that? I'm shocked that they would lock him in. I'd like to help him escape.

Stranger yet, I just realized that I'm calling this nearly transparent piece of bread Jesus... Why?

We leave the church. It's the first time I'm in a crowd without looking for a fight. The Brit I nearly smacked comes up to me:

"So, brother, did you like it?"

There he goes again. Dork! I answer:

"Yeah, it's strange. Very strange. Funny, even..."

He must think I'm a little off and leaves without a word.

Chapter 20

A Little Priest in My Wide World

That evening with Jesus and the handicapped kids got me all turned around. What's going on? Over the next month I don't win my fights as quickly as I used to. I hope Jesus isn't turning me into a girly.

To top it all off, on that memorable evening of kneeling before Jesus, Karine, one of the girls working at l'Arche, offers to take me home after our visit to the church. I left my bike at the house. "Thanks, Karine, you don't have to," I say.

She insists. She wants to see my place. I don't want her to. I'm still living in the cabin on the worksite, with its bunk beds and porno posters. I try to dissuade her. No luck.

"You really want to see my third-rate Hilton? Well, let's go then. You're in for a good one..."

She drives. We park along the fence line. A little worried, she asks where we are. We enter the worksite, I open the door to the trailer and invite her in. It's a harsh winter. The room is freezing and lit up by a single bulb. Showing her around doesn't take long. I'm embarrassed by the porno "wallpaper." I can tell that Karine has a pure heart and I don't want to shock her. I especially don't want her to judge me for this pad that smells so much of male loneliness. She insisted on coming... I like her. Karine isn't like other girls. There's something bright in her, she's gentle and determined at the same time.

I don't want to leave her. We go out for some ice cream. We talk. She's from a Jewish background and became Catholic at l'Arche where she's in charge of one of the homes. She wants to dedicate her life to serving the less fortunate and dreams of going to Honduras to open another branch of l'Arche. Honduras? I know Honduras, thanks to Monsieur Léon. I haul out the big guns and start showing off with a complete introduction to the country. I impress her, and impress her. It's weird, I don't feel like flirting with her.

I see Karine often. She's not afraid of my big tough guy act. Her friendship isn't about flattery or submission. It's just right. I like her. A really nice girl, one you wouldn't think of trying to seduce. One evening, as she's dropping me off at the "house," we come across Mohamed. I introduce them, we chat for a bit. Once Karine is gone, knowing his strong penchant for women, I ask my Algerian friend:

"What do you think of her?"

He's as taken as I am. When I explain to him that she wants to give her life to the poor in Honduras, he says: "Oh, wow!" and, after a sigh: "Now that's some girl." Mohamed confirms my impression; I'm happy.

In September of 1975, Karine takes off for Honduras to go live among the shanties of Tegucigalpa. I'm outraged by her leaving. For once I had found a girl that was out of the ordinary, one that wasn't a prostitute or one of those easy girls with their doe-eyed look, and she splits! She's going off to live with poor people half way across the world. What about me? Aren't I poor?

As the days go by, my anger subsides. I start realizing how fortunate I am, considering the rough path I've been on, to have met this flame that has changed my rather bleak view of women. Karine was my first Christian sister.

Just before her flight, she entrusts me to Fernand, who's like a brother to her. He's a big guy, also from l'Arche, plays rugby and coaches the kids. Everybody calls him Toto. I like him right off. He likes parties and has a good heart. He calls me "little brother" and it doesn't even bother me. We go up against each other in rugby. He's got some good friends, real men, straight up guys.

Toto tries to knock a little sense into me. He's got his work cut out for him. When I start acting like an idiot, he helps me out with the patience of an angel. Sometimes I fly off the handle, but he's always there waiting for me.

My gang's up to about eighty members now. We spread all the way out to Maubeuge and Pontoise to crash a party here and there. I deal a little on the side: a little extra padding on top of what my victories bring in.

The folks at l'Arche are poor, and their way of life never ceases to amaze me. I go there regularly to try and understand their bizarre planet. I'm straddling two contradictory worlds that are being driven farther and farther apart. Within me is a complete split.

Several people from l'Arche have told me about a priest, named Thomas Philippe, who founded l'Arche together with Jean Vanier. He lives in Trosly. They say his heart burns with love for all those who've suffered through their lives. "You'll see, he's a saint! You have to go see him," they tell me.

"A saint like Don Bosco and Vincent de Paul?" I ask.

"Yes, that's right, a man overflowing with love."

I decide to go see this Saint of Trosly. In an illustrated version, I discovered the lives of Don Bosco and Saint Vincent when I was fourteen. I couldn't get enough of them. I read them and reread them. Each time they brought tears to my eyes. The one is a force of nature who spent his life helping street kids, showing them circus tricks, and whose own mother washed and ironed their clothes! The other had assumed the hell of the galleys, taking the place of another rower, bought slaves their freedom and taken in abandoned children. Real heroes!

So I head off to see "saint" Thomas Philippe, imagining all the while I'm on my way to meet Don Bosco. On arriving in Trosly, I ask around.

"The priest? He's celebrating a Mass."

As I enter the chapel at l'Arche, it's time for communion. I make my way to the end of the line. I find myself standing in front of a little guy, dressed in priestly garb, his face is creased, a ring of dark hair crowns his bald head, like the monks on boxes of Camembert. "The body of Christ," he says as he hands me the host, thinking I'm there to take communion. As I touch his shoulder—that's the way street kids say hi—I feel the knot of his collarbone. He's frail. I'm disappointed. This Thomas is just a little man, nearly shriveled up, and I'm thinking to myself: "That's not a saint!" He's just a scaled down version next to the colossal Don Bosco. The saints are tough guys, they're strong, impressive and good looking. I know, I've spent days among them at the Saint-Riquier Abbey, restoring statues of John the Baptist, Peter, Jude and Stephen. There aren't any shrimps like Thomas Philippe.

Surprised, the priest remains still, holding the host in his hand. I turn my back on him and exit the chapel. I start walking toward my bike, intent on leaving the place, when a big gangly handicapped kid shows up and starts showing me his bicycle, all proud.

"My name's Didier. Don't you think I have a nice bike?"

He laughs as he speaks, full speed, swallowing his words, catching his saliva. I can't make out what he's mumbling and I couldn't really care less about his bike. He's insistent:

"Look at my bike, look at my bike!"

Fine, I'll look at Didier's bike. He spends his time shining it up. I don't have much of a choice, he's not about to let me go. Just then, Father Thomas walks out. He's headed in my direction. I dodge his gaze and start heading toward my bike parked a little further down. He follows me. I'm uneasy. He looks funny to me in his white robe.[1] I find this little bit of a man intimidating. Underneath his bushy eyebrows, his gaze is soft and kind.

With one kick I start up my bike. He comes up to me and starts talking shop. I'm surprised. My friends from l'Arche warned me: "He's a major brain, tops in philosophy and theology, one of the smartest guys on the planet"—along with a bunch of other superlatives. And here's the "major brain" taking an inter-

1. Father Thomas Philippe (1905-1993) was ordained to the priesthood at twenty-four years of age. He was a Dominican. This eminent theologian and great mystic was, together with Jean Vanier, a co-founder of l'Arche, in 1963, at Trosly-Breuil. The locals called him "the White Father," since he visited the sick and others in need on his bicycle, wearing his white Dominican's robe. [Ed.]

est in my bike! I'm thinking to myself: "I'm going to get you now."

"Father, would you like to go for a spin?"

"Oh, sure, I'd love to."

Darn! He got me. I thought he was going to back out. I can't weasel out of it. He hops on behind me and I holler:

"Hang on!"

We start up, full throttle. I'm thinking: "You got me my little man, but you're going to regret it! Here I am with a monk in a white robe on the back of my bike—I hope my buddies don't see me! Between the priest and all the handicapped kids, I'm hanging out with a pretty odd crowd these days. In the meantime, padre, you're not going to forget this little trip for a while!"

We tear down the road to Compiègne without much regard for the speed limit. In town, I take him on the little rodeo ride I set up to lose the cops or to impress the chicks: down a set of stairs, slalom along the sidewalk, popping a wheelie going the wrong way up one-way streets, burning red lights, speeding down the outer loop... It's the perfect circuit for sending chills down the spine of my latest conquest. Behind me, I can feel the little priest hanging on. He's not saying anything. He must be turning green and scared to death.

We get back on the road to Trosly, heading through the forest. He points out a little house near the chapel. I stop. He gets off. With a touch of sarcasm I ask:

"So, did you like the ride?"

He opens his squinting, tearing eyes and in his soft voice says: "It was nice, very pleasant!"

I'm floored. As I'm sitting there wondering what could possibly impress this guy, he takes my hand, places it in his withered palm and, as gently as ever, offers:

"Wouldn't you like Jesus' forgiveness?"

I stare at him with a huge question mark on my face:

"Forgiveness...? What are you talking about?"

He lets go of my hand, takes a step back, thinks for a second and says these magic words:

"It could do you some good..."

I'm just an unfortunate hoodlum, it would be dumb not to take every chance on something that might do me some good. I'm up for clearing out the racks if I have to.

He takes my hand again. All of a sudden, I realize I'm not even Christian. I pull my hand back:

"Wait, I'm not even on your side. I'm nothing! Not even baptized..."

He looks at me, surprised. He puts his left hand on my heart:

"Jesus knows your heart. Speak to him softly in your heart. He knows you and he loves you."

You don't need an engineering degree to understand that. The priest closes his eyes. I do the same. It's kind of dull in the dark, so I open my eyes. I look at him. His eyes are closed, his lips forming silent words. He's beautiful.

I've never thought of a man as beautiful before. And he's no Newman or Redford or Schwarzenegger either. "Whoa, Tim. You're going overboard there!"

He opens his eyes, full of light, and says:

"I can tell that you're alright."

It's true, I'm feeling pretty good. I've even got this strange, peaceful sensation.

As I'm about to leave, he takes me by the arm and says:

"Come and see me whenever you want to, the key's right here. Take care of yourself!"

I take off, a little muddled by the encounter and that prayer. I've got to meet my gang about seventy-five miles away to make the rounds at the nightclubs and get my footwork back. It's Saturday night here on earth. I'm not even Christian yet and here I go being a hypocrite... I'm trying to come up with an alibi for being two and a half hours late. I'm sure as heck not going to tell my tattooed bunch I went to Mass and rode around on my bike with a priest who gave me Jesus' forgiveness!

No need to lie, they didn't even ask. During the party, around four in the morning, my hazy conscience comes up with this idea: "What if I went to see Father Thomas? He said I could come whenever I wanted to, so let's go!" I'll find out if he really meant it or if it was just talk. That's how I test out all my future friends.

I sort them out so I don't have to worry about the fakers.

I leave my buddies and head for Trosly. Riding by night, full speed. The village is asleep. I find the key where he said it would be, but the door's open. I tiptoe inside. The little priest is sleeping, peaceful, trusting. I come near his bed. He wakes up, unafraid. He puts his feet on the floor and smiles. With a little sly look, his eyes sparkling at four in the morning, he asks me:

"You still want Jesus' forgiveness?"

I thought I'd make a crack. Not even close. He welcomes me like a father welcomes his son.

This priest has got me totally floored.

Chapter 21

Forgiveness Shock Therapy

Thomas Philippe, my little priest.

I get the urge to see him just like I get the urge to pee. It comes to me just like that, in the morning, and I take off for Trosly. Every time, Father Thomas gives me Jesus' forgiveness. That's how I receive the most amazing gesture of love, completely freely given, as simply as sharing a drink, without really realizing what it is I'm living. It works invisibly, putting me back together.

I like watching the father pray, his eyes closed. I call him father because that's what he is. He went from being a pal to being a friend; I chose that friend to be my father. I had a violent father. In the person of this priest, God is giving me a merciful father who holds me close. He radically changes my notion of what a father is. I'm starting to be able to imagine the idea of a God as Father without necessarily needing to be thrown down. I think to myself:

"If God is infinite, he must be better than Father Thomas… Is that even possible? That would be incredible!"

My heart is overwhelmed by these encounters. Little by little I start feeling my hatred for my biological father melt away. I'd like to hold on to it, to keep the flame of vengeance burning. It made me live, kept me standing, made me hit harder. I don't want to let go of it. But in spite of myself, I can feel it waning within me. What's happening?

I wasn't welcome in my family, I was violently rejected. My thirst for vengeance is strong enough for me to want to kill my father. Father Thomas heals these wounds by opening his arms to me: he's started an IV drip of love in my heart that's beginning to transform me.

With every encounter comes Jesus' forgiveness. Moments of peace.

I say nothing to the priest, nothing to Jesus. I keep my big mouth shut. Father Thomas prays silently beside me, one hand on my shoulder. I always open my eyes before he does, to see him pray. I turn into an insatiable consumer of mercy. A forgiveness-bulimic. Father Thomas' little house is my love filling station. I come and fill up as often as I can.

One day, as I'm getting my cardio-oil-and-lube job, someone comes and knocks on the window. Father opens up and says:

"Just a minute, please!"

Father Thomas' "minutes" are known for their elastic properties, tending more toward thirty minutes than sixty seconds. There's a line in front of his house. People come from far away to ask for his advice, compassion and comfort. His visitors represent a broad range of appearances, life experiences, social classes and cultures.

Suddenly something clicks in my head, like shock therapy to my sinful soul seeing this man granting these "accordion minutes" to everyone. He gives his life, every little minute of his life, opening his door to any who come knocking on it, even at four in the morning. He's open to everyone, all the time. He lets everyone feed off of him, humble, subtle and as radiant as a host.

The young showoff that I am is suddenly overwhelmed by this saint. This conductor for God who helps others enter the Kingdom without asking for tickets or even a baptismal certificate. He welcomed me straight out of my hole, without judging my appearance, without passing my leather jacket, my sooty jeans or my long braid through a propriety filter and social labeling. He took me on a first-class trip in a high-speed train to meet God the Father, the living God, the God of love. He makes me want to know Him and to start asking questions about life's meaning. He treats my ignorance with respect. He answers my questions with infinite patience. Without ever judging.

Sometimes I go after him, pouring out all my objections, I fight; I don't want to be convinced so easily:

"If your God is love, Father, why is there the suffering of abandoned children, or the suffering of a woman who sees her son die?"

Sometimes he answers with words, sometimes with silence. Often, he says nothing and stares at the crucifix.

One day, he says:

"Jesus didn't give an answer to every question. His apostles and the crowds that followed him weren't capable of hearing it all. We have to accept that we don't have answers to all our questions. That doesn't keep us from listening to all the questions people ask..."

The more I receive Jesus' forgiveness, the more I find myself confronted with the reality of my inner being: I have to change my way of life. There's no way for me to rebuild my life on the "values" that have kept me alive so far: vengeance, suspicion, violence... This is a path I know nothing about. The real struggle lies here. It's just beginning.

Little by little, Father Thomas quiets my inner turmoil and heals my wounds through forgiveness. He's a real missionary for the living God, an apostle of fire. An extraordinary ordinary human being. I had been wounded by Christians and by priests. Now, through him, I've begun to love them.

For a year, I go see him every day for five minutes. I want to change when I'm with him. I sense the enormity of the task ahead of me. I don't lose hope. He comforts me and reassures me just by his presence. Sometimes my desire for conversion crumbles. I lose it. He never worries. He welcomes me unconditionally. He must be in the image of God who's always dropping one notch further down just so the guy who's falling will land in his arms.

In my misery, Father Thomas, in all his goodness, is always one step ahead of me. He's always the one to offer me forgiveness. I'm too poor to ask for it.

From him, I receive three treasures: an unconditional welcome, forgiveness and hope.

I've come from the void and have nothing but darkness in my heart. Amidst this morass, this little priest, as gnarled as a grapevine, frail looking but with a soul as solid as a rock, began by scattering a few stars. Then he helped bring about the dawn of hope. Now he sows within me the conviction that I was made for the blessedness of love, for an everlasting love, and that it's even within the reach of a hoodlum. He takes me the way I am, without trying to change me. This priest is a channel of love.

Hope isn't something that comes from waving a magic wand. Willing men, women, children and elderly people struggle against the despair that has gripped the world and give hope a chance to grow. You can't walk by them without noticing it. They're radiant. Big questions don't come from ideas, they come from people and their ways of going about life.

Only actions can reverse the spiral of violence. Acts of peace and gestures of love set down in truth. A generosity that expects nothing in return defuses rage and extinguishes the flames of vengeance.

One day, you'll remember this gift that was given to you, and you won't lose hope.

God gave me a tremendous gift in Father Thomas.

The day he became my father, I wanted to become a part of his family. I've decided to become a Christian. As I speak with him about it, he's overjoyed and his eyes flutter with delight.

Nonetheless, there's still one objection I want to put to him, something that's got me bothered, if I may say so:

"How do you handle your sexuality? For me, if I don't get laid, my balls hurt... what about you?"

He presses his lips together, looking for the right words, and says very naturally:

"Your sexuality is like your bike. To get down the stairs, you had to practice, you fell, you got up, you took the time and ultimately mastered the thing. On that day, you were really happy... Controlling your sexuality doesn't happen in a day, nor in fifteen.

It's a series of small acts of self-control. And what a joy it is when you can make it down those stairs!"

Evidently, he didn't forget our little escapade. I keep going:

"I've got too many bad driving habits! I've got women under my skin..."

"You mean you got into the habit of popping Wheelies when the light turns green? To change that, you're going to have to become aware of your habits. Then you'll try at least one time to start up keeping your front wheel on the ground. You can catch on the first time. After that, it's all down hill... Try it, you'll see."

I'd never even thought of that. I'm amazed and full of hope. He didn't completely answer my question though:

"What about you, Father? What do you make of your sexuality, since you're not allowed to use it?"

He looks at me affectionately, rises and goes to pull a book out of his library.

"Read this, you'll understand. I'll lend it to you."

I leave him, his tome under my arm. It's called *The Mystical Love of St. John of the Cross and St. Teresa of Avila*. I'm not sure this book is going to shed any light on my questions. Regardless, that same night, I try and dive into it. It feels like I'm reading Latin. I have no idea what this is talking about.

A week later, crestfallen as ever, I return the book, still with no solution to my problem:

"Your masterpiece is a bunch of nonsense, Father. First of all, it may as well be in Latin, and for me, that's not at all the way it is! I like women, Father, I really like women!"

He smiles, thinks for a moment, considers how different I am and offers me forgiveness.

When it's time for me to leave, he tells me he loves me, and as if he were entrusting me with a secret, he adds:

"Always strive for what is most beautiful."

This unsolicited expression of pure affection overwhelms my heart. So few people dare to give this tremendous gift of happiness: to know that one is loved and to hear it spoken. It's like a magic potion against violence, anger and rebellion.

Day after day, his homeopathic treatment transforms me. I become a "convert." A fool for God, in every sense of the word. For others, it's not all that relaxing. I'm on fire, I want to live the Gospel to a tee and rebuild the Church, like St. Francis of Assisi. I find that Catholics don't do enough.

Janine, a close friend of Father Thomas, knows how to temper my mystical escapades. This woman is sharp, she has the heart of an artist and knows how to listen to people of all different backgrounds and draw the best out of each one. Unlike some others at l'Arche who are somewhat leery of me, she offers me her trust. It's a precious gift. In my inner hit parade, Janine is right behind Father Thomas Philippe who gets the Golden-Heart award.

She's in charge of "the Farm," the reception and prayer home at l'Arche, in Trosly-Breuil, where Father Thomas lives. In the yard there's a small trailer that she's put at my disposal. It's my new palace. A room of my own, just for me! I feel like a prince in this little space of mine that helps me slowly get back into the flow of things.

Those in charge of l'Arche are aware of my skills and offer me odd jobs. My life is spent between boxing—having since gone pro—and Trosly, where I work here and there fixing up the different houses. I try to stay away from the gang and its shady activities. I want to change my life.

At l'Arche, I find food for my heart and begin rebuilding myself; at the gym, I calm the flaming passions I harbor. I'm finding myself more and more detached from the sport. My only reason for boxing—to exact revenge from my father—is starting to fade. I'm realizing that the more I fight against my violent past, the more violent I become. I have to learn to love that past. That's going to be my great struggle.

In the home, I shock a good number of people. Father Thomas protects me. There's no doubt, I'm unpredictable. Growing up without an inner framework has given my impulses free reign. Taking advantage of a fight in some foreign country, I take off suddenly. A few days later, they find me shooting a pistol at the pigeons nesting under the chapel roof at l'Arche, and giving lessons to some of the new assistants. That doesn't keep me from making some space and caring for sick and wounded animals that win my affection.

Sometimes my past catches up to me when I'm hurt in the present. In a second, my blue skies grow dark and stormy.

One afternoon, I get a serious case of angst. My friend Martine stood me up. This lively, graceful Parisian comes to help out three times a week. She promised to give me a French lesson at three o'clock and I've been waiting for her for half and hour. At 3:30 I hop on my bike and take off, steaming. I go back to see my pals. They give me a warm, even emotional welcome, like old war buddies reminiscing. We don't want to split up. We steal some chickens, some ducks, some rabbits and organize a country roast. The party lasts all night.

At five in the morning, I gather the few birds that escaped the feast to take them to Father Thomas. The sun's coming up. On his doorstep, with all this loot squawking away in my hands, I suddenly realize the depth of my stupidity. I wake him up. He takes me in and, noticing the animals, says:

"Do you want me to give them the blessing of St. Francis of Assisi?"

"No Father, don't joke about it, this is serious."

"What's so serious?"

He sits me down and listens to me, bemused, tapping my hand.

"That's not so serious. At least it's not a station wagon!"

"A station wagon? What's a car got to do with my chickens and my doldrums?"

"I'm sorry, I'll explain. One of the people who passed through here and stayed at the home in the village stole a station wagon. All I'm saying is that everything is relative and that you mustn't judge yourself more harshly than the Lord would. Loving oneself is the hardest thing to do."

He gives me Jesus' forgiveness; I was expecting to be judged and abandoned.

That morning, through my father's kindness and patience, I come to understand that Jesus won't leave me hanging out to dry and that he'll forgive the dumb mistakes of my troubled past. Come to think of it, I want to be a part of the Church, of the big family. I accept everything, even obedience, I'll take it all, I have a thirst for everything.

I want to join the Christian gang.

I go to the director of l'Arche and give her my application to work as an assistant in one of the homes. I'm a stone sculptor, a skilled artisan, now I want to become a Christian apprentice. She gives me a kind smile and says:

"We can take a closer look in a year."

I'm devastated. I'm working trying to patch up my life and my scaffolding just collapsed. I decide to change, to convert, and I get a condescending: "No, not right away!" I could be dead in a year, little lady! Do you realize how much trouble you can get into in a year?

That day, I swear at God and his gang. This lady gets an earful. You want to turn your life around but the old Christians, the ones who know the secret, the treasure, the Word of God, they stick your head under water instead of extending a helping hand! In my indignation, I scream:

"It's all a bunch of hot air; nothing but words!"

I leave l'Arche, furious and outraged. I'll never set foot here again, I swear. You can't go taking me for some kind of idiot.

A year and a half later I would realize that, in doing what she did, the director had actually rendered me a tremendous service.

Chapter 22

Age Twenty-One
My First Birthday Present

I quit my gang of buddies and I've just been dumped by my Christian friends. I find myself marginalized in both worlds. Once again, I'm alone, wandering through Paris, mulling over my bitterness and outrage.

I can feel the tentacles of my past reaching through me, pushing me to despair. They worm their way around, tightening their grip, they start choking me. "No, you'll never be able to change..."

After three days of wandering aimlessly, I happen upon a hitchhiker near Porte d'Orléans, his pack at his feet and his thumb in the air. I think to myself: "Hey, why not? I'll give it a shot." I stick my thumb out. Another hitchhiker comes at me:

"Hey, you were the last one here, get in line over there. This isn't your spot!"

What's up with this guy, getting on my case and all? I start toward him thinking I'm going to lift more than my thumb when I remember that I made a promise to God. I grumble my way to the end of the line.

"You can thank God, you doof..."

I haven't even got my thumb up when a clunker pulls up. The driver, a Viking-hippie-peace-and-love type asks me:

"Where are you headed?"

I stuck my thumb out to hitch a ride, but I hadn't really given any thought to what would come after that, so I say:

"What about you, where are you going?"

"Totézé."

Say what? Totézé? Destination unknown. Or maybe I misunderstood. I'm thinking: "He must be from the sticks, he's got some kind of dialect, like me." I keep trying:

"And what are you planning on doing in Totézé?"

"Camping."

"Alright, I'm in."

"You don't have a backpack?"

"No, nothing. I don't have anything."

...Nothing but my bare hands stuffed in my worn pockets. My chauffeur is part of the generation that did '68. He's a bit of a nut, but he's nice, peaceful. After five hours on small roads, we clank our way into a small village in Burgundy named Taizé. He says:

"Here we are!"

I get that Totézé has nothing to do with a dialect; it's "to Taizé." A dinosaur would have caught on quicker...

In this little village near Cluny, in Burgundy, an ecumenical religious community has settled, preaching peace, reconciliation and fraternal gatherings. Young people from every country come together in a very "cool" atmosphere. L'Arche gave me a taste of this kind of atmosphere. I get along with everyone. I've joined a group of fantastic Italians and Belgians. Among them is Fredo, a sixteen-year-old handicapped kid. I find myself completely taken with him. His legs won't support him anymore, so I carry him around in my arms, along with his wheel chair that keeps getting stuck in the mud building up between the tents. It's also a way for me to keep busy during prayer time. For someone as restless as I am, they always seem to go on forever. It keeps me busy and helps me keep my bearings.

On the eve of my farewell, in early September, Fredo asks me: "Would you come to my house in Belgium for Christmas?"

I pretend to think it over and answer:

"Well, for Christmas I'm already booked, but I could come on December 27th."

Christmas is my enemy. Family traditions when you don't have a family are a bit hard to take. You see the presents under the tree and your host, trying to be nice, starts showing you around: "Come see the tree and the pretty lights. This one's for my dad, this one's for my mom. Look at what my grandparents gave me! And my godfather..." You don't say a thing. Not only do you not have any presents, you don't even have a father, or a mother, or grandparents... First the outrage at being different hits, and then you just feel like breaking things. Christmas gets me a little bent out of shape!

So I leave Fredo with a promise:

"We're on for December 27th, then. Ciao!"

Four months later, right on time, I arrive in Brussels. I find my handicapped friend and spend three wonderful days in his home. He's also living in one of the homes of l'Arche that was founded in the Belgian capital by a priest. After these few days, as I'm getting ready to leave for who knows where, this priest, Father Roberty, asks me:

"You wouldn't want to stay here a while and help me out, would you? I need some men."

As I'm thinking as quickly as possible, he adds:

"I think you were sent by the Holy Virgin."

I burst out laughing and say:

"Let me show you my pedigree and you can tell me if you still think I was sent by the Holy Virgin!"

I give him an overview... O.K., so I converted, but I still haven't lost all my twisted habits:

"One day, I'm all fired up, screaming my love for God on the rooftops, making resolutions, all gung-ho... the next, I forget everything and fall flat!"

Father Roberty, a tall, good-looking man, listens to me attentively. I see tears in his eyes and remember my judge. I think to myself: "That's odd, a judge and a priest tearing up as they listen to me!" I'm touched and find myself taking a liking to this priest. I answer:

"Alright, I'm your man. If I can be of service..."

I would spend a year and a half in the service of the handicapped residents of La Branche, every once in a while helping out also at

La Ruche, another home. I carry my new brothers and sisters around, dress, wash, and feed them as well as take them to the bathroom and on walks. I pray with them in these liturgies that they're so fond of. I'm their legs and arms; they're the catalyst for my reconstitution. As I see it, this is a tremendous step up, an immeasurable gift.

In the morning, when it's time to get up, there's always music in every heart. Except for Jean-Paul. As a climber, he conquered the Himalayas then became paralyzed by a stupid fall in a cave right near his home. Soon after that, his wife was killed in a car accident. He lost everything, even his mobility. He's completely dependent on his wheelchair. When I go to wash him in the morning, he complains bitterly, brooding over his suffering. Sometimes he gets discouraged and depressed and gives up.

One day, I bawl him out:

"Jean-Paul, cut the crap! You complain about not being able to do anything by yourself, not even getting to the bathroom. All you've got to do is build your arms up some and you'd be able to get yourself out of your chair and have some privacy."

That shakes him up. His answer: "Bingo!" He starts building his arms and shoulders with daily exercises. To help him train, I strap myself in a chair, like him, and lift the same weights.

Three months later, he's washing himself, dancing to rock music popping wheelies in his chair, driving a car and folding his wheelchair all by himself.

Six months later, he's got the arms of a lumberjack and gotten back to studying. Now Jean-Paul is an interpreter and weight-lifting champion.

He plays the DJ for dance parties at the home and everyone has a great time. I'm sure God brought us together so we could help each other. I helped him out, but Jean-Paul's efforts and dreams are a silent motivation for me. When I feel like throwing in the towel, he laughs and says:

"Tim, you're always encouraging us to fight and then when some woman gets on your nerves you just take off? That's low. Come on, tough it out. Plus, I love you. Doesn't that count for anything?"

Well sure, with that kind of argument... Thanks for setting me straight, Jean-Paul. Following his advice, I go talk things over with the lady that was getting on my nerves. We talk for a bit then, to top things off, I pick her up and dump her fully clothed into a bathtub. Everyone cracks up and the problem's over. It's like a baptism for a fresh start.

I would end up staying in Belgium in this home at l'Arche for a year and a half. An extraordinary period of growth. I had been an intractable, proud, macho champion, with the world revolving around me; I've learned to serve those who are weaker than I am. It's mind-boggling! The handicapped are my masters. I obey them. Don't get me wrong, my temperament has a really hard time keeping up. It's an inner struggle for me to accept this discipline, this humility.

One night, I'm wakened several times to take people down to the bathroom. Finally at my wit's end, worn out, I start losing it:

"If one more person rings, I'm dropping them from the top of the stairs!"

Naturally, another voice calls out. I get up. I go to her bed and take this girl in my arms. She wonders why I'm taking so long to get her situated. I step up to the railing and, as I'm about to toss her from the top of the stairs, I feel her little misshapen arm around my neck. Suddenly I realize that these handicapped kids show me signs of affection that I never got from my parents.

So I take her to the bathroom and head back to bed with a splitting headache. When you keep anger bottled up inside, it's bound to show up on the outside: in my case it flows right through the coffee pot.

The next day, as I'm going about my business in the home, my attention is drawn to an odd sound coming from the other side of a door. It sounds like something clicking at regular intervals. Tick... tick... tick... I walk into the room to find Frédéric, a severely handicapped little boy, trying to work a typewriter. His face is deformed, the left side of his mouth is twisted and his eyes tend to roll around in his head. I kind of like Frédéric. In the morning he runs his hand through my hair to say hello. Sometimes his muscles give out, his hand gets away from him and he pulls on my hair or head-butts me accidentally. In spite of his handicap that prevents any verbal communication, Frédéric has found a new way to interact with the others: a typewriter.

I had never seen him type. It's kind of surreal. Here's this decrepit little body in a wheelchair vehemently projecting itself toward the keyboard. It's a calculated leap, completely concentrated on reaching a single key, because he can only type one letter at a time. With a single finger on his twisted right hand, he buries the selected key. Then his entire body bounces back as if he were recoiling. After every strike, after each letter, the wheelchair rolls back a good meter, in preparation for another assault. This struggle is both magnificent and pathetic.

My first reaction is to think: "The kid's crazy, he can't leave this sorry machine alone! He's going to wear himself out... All this wasted energy, for nothing!" I go to take it from him. He grumbles and lets me know to leave him alone. I take a peek over his shoulder. Surprise: his note has got no mistakes, it even has periods and commas and everything. So I let him go about his business, composing his mysterious note.

Frédéric has been typing for two days. Every time I pass by his door, the ticking of his machine makes my heart ache and moves me with compassion. I imagine the movement to and fro of this little shriveled body. His indomitable desire for expression demands respect and admiration in its infinite patience. I feel ashamed as I remember the typewriter I demolished in one of the homes I passed through, all because I couldn't find the third letter of my name on the keyboard...

I find it odd that the suffering of others is able to tear at my heart and shred me inside even though I've never admitted to myself that I could also suffer.

On the evening of August 9th, Frédéric rolls his wheelchair over to me before dinner. I detect a look of playful mischief in his eyes. He comes up to me and, as much as he's able, with his arms all folded in on themselves, stretches out his hand to give me a piece of paper. It's a note, five lines long. This is what his typing frenzy was all about. Five lines written in two days of harrowing strikes, two days of going up and back within his wheelchair, two days of intense concentration.

Five lines to wish me a happy birthday. Five lines of love. The first birthday present I've ever had. I grab my letter of love and make off like a bandit up to my room. I put on my boxing gloves—they're all I have left of my past—and reread his poem. He tells me things no one has ever dared tell me.

Before this gift I suddenly recoil. Frédéric caught me by surprise. His gesture got past my guard. I'm scurrying, trying to defend myself against this unexpected intrusion of love. I'm even furious for having received something without giving anything in return. I don't like that. I'm usually the one to do the giving. I even shower people with gifts. I've won a lot of money boxing and I show off with gifts. I love to see my friends' eyes light up when I hand them my presents.

Up in my room, I release my anger against a chunk of wood. The rage gives way to a tremendous void. I sit on the edge of my bed and stare at these five lines. It isn't the most stylish bit of writing, it isn't great literature, but it's straight from the heart. From its very depths. There's nothing flimsy about it.

Frédéric never would have made front page news or gotten into the top magazines. It's disturbing just to see the way he looks. And yet Frédéric is an Apollo of love. What loving patience he must have needed to write this letter! He suffers from humiliation for his inability to speak. The only word he manages to articulate from time to time is "po-ta-to." Three syllables that demand a tremendous effort on his part. Whenever he's looking you in the eyes, "po-ta-to" means "I love you!"

A lot of people think that a Frédéric is something that ought to be gotten rid of. I thank God he hasn't fallen prey to the narrow vision of those in good health. With all of his sixteen years of a "ruined life," as some so easily conclude, Frédéric has understood the most important part of life: love freely given, effort and generosity. For me, that represents a way of life. This gift brings me to my knees in my heart. As I stare at this letter, these five lines of love, my eyes well up, my throat stings and my anger gives way to tears. I start bawling like a child. My life has just taken a major turn.

Father Thomas only bawled me out once: when I turned down a gift someone was trying to give me. He took my hand, saying:

"Never say no to a gift, you could stifle that person's generosity. It could keep them from growing and discourage them. Through that gift, God is asking us to be sufficiently humble to receive it, to accept the other person's ability to give and allow it to grow within them."

Love is a boomerang: you get much more than you give. Knowing how to receive is as important as knowing how to give.

Try as I may to stem the flow of tears by calling myself a "girly," there's no slowing the watershed. The tears keep coming. After a few long minutes, the well starts drying up, my eyes begin to clear. I start thinking. Frédéric found the means to make something beautiful out of his existence. His physical handicap doesn't serve as an excuse to avoid creating a life of love. I suffer from a different handicap. My childhood is what was twisted, not my body. And when I want to forget the turmoil of my past, an underlying violence grabs me by the throat. My beloved "adrenaline" demands to flow through my veins again. Rage turns my eyes into a pair of slits, full of hatred. I see nothing but red and start pounding.

I want to change, to show signs of love, to see others through the eyes of love. I want to turn my life into a life of love.

I want to blend beauty and goodness into my life.

My handicapped friends show me the way. The Little Way. Their greatest gift is their life.

I receive it on my knees within my heart.

From now on I'm faced with a struggle that I'll never win.

Chapter 23

My Friends in Suffering

Five lines have just turned my life upside down.

I wasn't loved. Then I'll start loving others the way I want to be loved. If I wait to receive something before giving anything, I'll be waiting forever. From now on, my struggle will be to live what I was kept from living.

I'll see others the way I would like them to see me: with love, patience and compassion instead of with the belligerent gaze of a survivor, sharpened like a blade. I'm going to learn how to give with my heart.

That's it, I've decided.

Suddenly, those unbearable words that poisoned my childhood start rising like putrid bubbles within my memory: "It's genetic, beaten children end up beating their children," "It's genetic, children of alcoholics end up drinking," "It's genetic, abandoned children end up abandoning their children," "It's genetic, children whose parents are separated will end up separated..."

"And regardless, my dear, the apple never falls far from the tree! Poor kids, 75 to 80% of them will just repeat their parents' dysfunctions. They can't help it, it's genetic!"

At night, in my room, alone with God, I decide to make my life belie my genetic makeup, to close the door on my past and to clean out my memory. From now on I won't listen to people who know everything or to any of the crap from people who spread despair.

It is possible to start fresh; you just have to be determined.

Loving others means not only telling them they're beautiful but also that they have what it takes to make it. It means telling the battered and bruised: "You're wonderful." It means also saying: "Don't fear yourself or your past, don't fear your parents. You're free, you can change, you can rebuild your life." To love means to believe that every person that bears painful memories or emotional or physical wounds can change that wound into a source of life. To love means to hope for others and to instill hope in them. There's nothing genetic about children who have been beaten or abandoned, or who have suffered from alcohol or drug abuse and other horrors. They all have the right to change.

It's important to remember the past, not to get bogged down in it, but to remain ever vigilant: no, I won't give in to the sirens of fate.

Let's take advantage of the fact that each one of us is unique. A simple sign of love, freely given, can shatter genetically dictated despair and overthrow the order of supposedly programmed chromosomes.

Frédéric's gift is an injection of hope. On this day, thanks to him, I've decided that I'll be married one day. And that I'll have children. Yes, I'll be married for life, not just to try it out while keeping the back door open so I can take off at the first sign of trouble or my first disappointment. I vow never to abandon my children. I'll give them what I never received.

I chose to dream large. I'm a show off and I don't mind talking myself up… when you start off really small, you may as well aim high.

On this evening of August 9th, in my own little space, I'm happy in my head and in my heart, as if the Good Lord had suddenly brought spring to birth inside me. What a birthday!

The next day, I'm high as a kite. Injected with love, high on life. I'm alive with a desire to do everything and to do it all in the best possible way.

But you can't change just like that, by flipping a switch in your head. Old habits die hard. In spite of the prince's orders, they stay on duty like rebel guards refusing to let positive resolutions past the gates.

Living together requires that we always remain attentive to the weather patterns in the hearts of others. I'm often deaf and clumsy. I inadvertently harm those close to me. How can I avoid causing such damage? One day, as I'm following the manufacturer's directions to try and put a dresser together, I check out the finished product, proud of my work, and suddenly realize: "Why didn't I think of that? A person is like a piece of furniture: there's an owner's manual, it's a little different depending on the model. To live in harmony with someone, you just have to be willing to ask them for their owner's manual and dare to give them yours."

All proud of my discovery, I try it out for a couple of weeks. I go to all those I spend time with and say:

"If I don't love you the way I ought to, tell me so I can change. If I do love you the way I ought to, tell me that too so I can keep it up. But don't tell me in six months, tell me right away so I don't waste any time!"

Love is like a mall. You have to try things on. Love others the way you would like to be loved. Look on them the way you would like others to look on you. Give the way you would like others to give to you. Try it for fifteen days. If you're not satisfied, simply return to sender...

Trying out love means adopting it. During the months following that exceptional birthday, my life would change dramatically. I find myself making friends with people from all over, from every background, every race and culture, rejecting any kind of label, looking for their differences. For me, these people are like a foreign country just waiting to be discovered: not so much an obstacle to be overcome as a mystery to be explored. I'm becoming a globe-trotter of differences. I'm a man with the freedom to love my own way, no longer a prisoner in my little village, nor of my small circle of relationships. I'm a galactic traveler. My friends are like my beloved forest in its variety of species. Trees with twisted branches let the light through much better than the ones with perfectly straight trunks.

Fresh air, blue sky! Whenever I find myself amazed by a person's heart, I want to get to know the soil and the culture that shaped him. Finding a friend makes me want to visit his home.

I'm off. I don't know exactly what I'm looking for. I crisscross Europe by hitching rides with truckers. I load and unload, I watch the truck while the driver takes a break. I ride along and hop out whenever I feel like it. Belgium, Holland, Sweden, Norway, Denmark, Italy, former Yugoslavia...

I like crossing borders. It's as if I were being symbolically freed from every limit that was imposed on me during my childhood. I like smiling at strangers, with no other way to communicate than expressions and simple gestures. I quickly realize I know nothing, but thanks to the kids that share a part of themselves, I learn that each one of them is a treasure. In Greece, in Turkey, in Lebanon, in Israel, in the United States, in Canada...

Throughout my wanderings with a pack on my back, the discovery of countries, people and various customs strengthens my faith in man. I'm overwhelmed by the hospitality of poor folks who take me in and share their everyday. When it comes down to it, there's only one question I'm interested in when I meet one of these brothers in mankind, and as I ask him, I place my hand on his chest: "How is your heart?"

It seems plain as day to me that there is no greater suffering than that lived by each one of us. Suffering has no social boundaries. You can recognize poor people. Their misery is draped over their shoulders like a coat. Extending your hand to them out of charity can turn into a gesture of love.

There are also people who seem very "proper," of whom you might ask: "How are you?" and they'll say "Fine." Trapped within themselves and bound to their social environment, they're unable to say anything else. They're incapable of expressing the suffering that's suffocating and shattering their lives. And we pass by, without seeing the distress in their eyes, without listening to the silence of their cries, without even noticing that their heart's barometer is reading "hurricane."

All these friends are like lights for me. Thanks to them, I realize that God isn't interested in the fraction of a second of tumbling when we human beings fall apart. God looks at the time we spend getting back up. The hours, the days, the months and the years when men and women attempt, imperceptibly, to become better people. Lives are like so many hidden treasures.

All too often, when looking at others, people stop at the fall.

We mustn't ever judge.

Four months after my birthday, a friend of mine invites me to her parents' home for Christmas Eve. The table is beautifully set, with porcelain plates and crystal glasses. Cathy's mother serves me a thick soup, then offers some to her husband. They address each other very formally. Their manner seems strange to me; I tag the two of them as a little "off." The dishes, each as delicious as the next, keep filing by in the midst of kindness and laughter when suddenly, in an overwhelming moment, I catch a gaze passing between this man and this woman. They may well be formal, but you can't mistake a look like that one, they love each other deeply. That night I understand that people are better off being formal and loving one another than they are being all casual and disregarding each other. Some formality brings people closer together, while there's a certain kind of familiarity that can be deadly.

After the midnight Mass, the father says:

"Let's go have some hot chocolate in the living room and you can see the tree."

The tree! This is terrible! I'm stuck, trapped. I can't turn him down. Damn tree! Lead-footed, I start making my way to the living room, dreading the moment. Inside my head, I'm screaming: "You never should have accepted this invitation. You know Christmas Eve isn't any good for kids without families!"

Just then, Cathy's mother says:

"Tim, I have something for you."

Did I hear that right? Yeah, she hands me a package wrapped in red paper and a golden bow. I open it slowly, carefully removing the wrapping paper. I remember the hospital and the wrapping paper that taught me how to walk and to draw. Inside there are three candles—one green, one yellow and one red—some soap and a beautiful box with "Skipper" engraved in it. I sit there, stunned, speechless. For me, this consideration is priceless. The Good Lord's got a sense of humor: there I was making fun of their differences and here they are spoiling me unexpectedly. Total surprise!

I spend the night with them, my Christmas present in my arms, like the child I would have liked to be.

Chapter 24

The Adventurers of God

One morning I arrive in Rome, at the Termini train station, always on the lookout for unusual encounters. On the sidewalk I see a tiny old lady wearing a strange white dress. She's hesitant to step into the arena and seems frightened by the rodeo of traffic going by. I walk up to her.

"Can I help you?"

She fixes her bright eyes on me—they're so light, set in her wrinkled face—and she smiles. She accepts, in English. We cross the street. She keeps hold of my arm. On the other side, she rings the doorbell of an apartment building. Three men answer together. Their faces light up.

"Oooh, Mother!" they exclaim.

The little lady holding my arm seems to have them mesmerized. An Indian fellow with dull skin says:

"Oh, how fortunate you are to be with Mother..."

The old woman interrupts him with a friendly tap on the arm. With her lovely smile she asks me to go with her to see some friends. I've got no plans, I'm totally in the moment. Let's go. I like this little lady, tall as a mushroom, wrinkled as a raisin and bossing men around. I follow her.

Everyone we visit throughout the afternoon tells me:

"You're so fortunate to be with Mother Teresa!"

I just shrug, not caring much about it and not knowing who Mother Teresa is. All I know is that this woman has a profoundly good heart, I can feel it. I have no way of guessing she's the mother of the poor and probably a saint. My knowledge of nuns is pretty limited. I stumble through some English and we have a good laugh, riding the Roman buses.

We get off at the Basilica of Santa Maria Maggiore. I greet a few homeless friends, Francisco, Bergam and Mario, from Naples. I introduce "Ma," as people like to call Mother Teresa. I see Mario enjoying a basket of food handed out by the Brotherhood of Charity, not realizing that she's the one who founded the order. As he intently peels his orange, he points out enormous steps to the basilica and says:

"Have a seat, there's plenty of room."

We burst out laughing and find our spot on the steps. Like any great Lord, Mario shares his orange with us. He's a great friend with a good heart. He's been living in the street for years. Whenever we disagree, he starts holding forth in some Neapolitan dialect while I come back with another from up North. These incomprehensible arguments always end in fits of laughter and a good "street chaser": a shot of wine.

We leave Francisco and Mario to go on to a series of somewhat more tedious visits. Some rich donors that she's going to thank. It never fails. They look at me enviously and say:

"Oh, how fortunate you are to be with Mother Teresa!"

My little Mother Teresa. She seems mighty tired. We walk in silence as she holds onto my arm. As time passes, she's more and more hunched over. But as soon as anyone speaks to her—it never ends, always more people—I can feel her body straighten up and her hand gripping more firmly. What energy in this woman! I'm thinking to myself: "Can't they leave her be? She's old, she's earned a little rest, give her a break!" She says nothing and faces these many visitors with joyful smile.

We leave the neighborhood of Termini and take the subway to Trefontana. Finally a bit of silence. We hike a dirt path along the outskirts of a men's monastery. At the top of the hill we come to a place overlooking a magnificent and surprising landscape: Vietnamese-type bungalows, spread out amidst a thick underbrush. An Eden basking in a light breeze. The humidity and bustle of Rome are far away.

A few nuns surround us and greet "Ma" with respect. She, in turn, introduces me to an attractive woman dressed in a denim robe, with a veil covering her hair. Her name is Mother Madeleine. She sounds my heart with her sonar-gaze and takes my hand to lead me. She's the first person all day who didn't tell me I was lucky to be with Mother Teresa. Her gentleness settles into my heart. We have tea together. The two women retreat to speak together. I move away.

As she's about to leave us, Mother Madeleine offers me a gift saying: "Come back and see me next time you're in Rome, promise?" I just nod because the words are stuck inside me. I'm highly intimidated by this adventurer of God. I open the box: it's a Baby Jesus made out of clay.

Mother Teresa gives me a hug and leaves in a car with her sisters. I get back to my freedom.

Only two years later would I realize my good fortune in that encounter. One evening, in Trosly, we're all watching a TV documentary about the Little Sisters of Charles de Foucauld. The nuns of this young congregation have chosen to live in abject poverty amidst shanties and in the suburbs. They're the loving presence of Christ among the poorest of the poor. The journalist is speaking with a beautiful nun, full of personality. She's the founder of the wonderful order. I cry out:

"But, I know her! That's Madeleine, my friend Madeleine!"

Of course, no one believes me, except for Father Thomas.

"I swear, that's the woman in Rome I was telling you about!"

The other helpers just laugh: "While you're at it, why don't you tell us you know Mother Teresa too!"

"Well, uh, actually, that's just it. Mother Teresa's the one who introduced me to Mother Madeleine..."

I stop talking. They're going to think I'm trying to pull one over on them. But still...

As macho as I am, I'm still impressed with these two women and their strong personalities, who went through so many hard times before finding their way. These pioneers braved every obstacle in their way as well as the inertia of institutions in order to remain faithful to their inner calling.

Mother Madeleine has become precious in my life. I go and see her from time to time in Rome; she's become my spiritual mother. She radiates a tender and peaceful presence. She's a female likeness of Father Thomas. Every time I leave her, I come away a better person. Mother Madeleine speaks so simply about Jesus, so lovingly and with such a passionate love that she could melt the icecaps in the hardest of hearts.

She treats me like one of her sons and spoils me when I'm about to leave, stuffing my bag full of cookies and sandwiches and always some spiritual reading to feed my endangered soul.

Her womanly gaze has changed my vision of women. Hers is a gaze full of beauty, goodness, respect and benevolent tenderness, awaiting nothing in return. My spiritual poverty isn't an obstacle for her. On the contrary.

"Only something empty can be filled; don't ever fill up on yourself," she says, one fist on her left hip.

What I also find amazing about these women, as with Father Thomas, is their chastity. These are pure beings, they're not playing around. And as pure as they are, they don't judge me. I'm impressed, especially since I'm such an avid babe consumer. In nightclubs, I get girls just like that. A lot of the time they'll play hard to get, but they aren't too disappointed when you serenade them with something other than a lullaby... sometimes I take them to the woods to listen to the bellow of a stag that, at times, sounds somewhat like a swan's song.

Joel is another friend of mine I find truly impressive. He's a surveyor I met during my internship. This guy's been engaged to a girl for five years. One day I'm teasing him about sex and he answers completely seriously:

"I've never touched Annie. We'll make love only once we're married. It's the most beautiful proof of my love I can give her."

That nearly bowled me over. I'm awestruck by this guy's purity and honesty!

I just try to tame the beast, without much success...

One day, as I'm leaving Father Thomas' place, full of positive resolutions, my bike breaks down and I have to thumb a ride back to Compiègne. A woman stops and picks me up. She's a doctor, we chat. Half an hour later, I'm in her bed with my resolutions tucked under the pillow. I can't help it! Filled with regret, I cry my heart out and ask Jesus' forgiveness with a promise never to do it again. Three hours later, I'm sitting out in front of a café having a beer, a whole new set of resolutions tallied up, when a girl comes up to me. We talk. She speaks to me from her heart. Again, I wind up in her bed. It's a curse and a sickness. I need a powerful injection to ward off depression.

I high-tail it back to see Father Thomas. No one's home. On the door is a note: "I've gone on a trip." I enter the old stone chapel next to his room. I sit down in an old beat up leather chair. I stare at the Blessed Sacrament resting on the altar, then at the icon of the Holy Virgin. I start talking to them, telling them very simply that I'm fed up with having my balls on fire and the endless string of chicks. I'm crying as I talk, talking as I cry, without anger, just tremendous anguish. I talk and then keep quiet, still sitting on Father's chair, facing God, and his Mother. The night goes by, then morning, then afternoon... A tremendous, silent void.

At the end of the day, just before the Mass with Father, who's just come home, on a whim I say to the Virgin Mary:

"I vow a year of abstinence. Love but no sex for a year, I promise!"

I don't know what got into me. My record's three days!

During Father's Mass, I wind up next to a beautiful girl, a new assistant at l'Arche. I've got a few choice words for the Blessed Virgin:

"My vow's off to a great start, thanks!"

I lower my gaze, close myself off and slip out at the end of the celebration.

"Could I talk to you?"

The girl came running after me. I say:

"No, I've got to set the table and I don't have time and..."

She's utterly disarming. She seems so completely pure.

"Well, alright, we could see each other after supper, I'm going to watch the deer at nightfall."

Inside, I'm cursing myself out: "You're nuts, you're totally setting yourself up! Don't forget you gave your word!"

That night we wander under the stars, without touching one another. We start again the next day. And the next. I beat my record! Victory! During this year of abstinence, I would discover the beauty of a friendship without ulterior motives and the joy of being able to give a girl the most beautiful gift a man can give her: respect.

My insatiable appetite for discoveries and encounters leads me on a trip to Canada to find my roots. I take a year's sabbatical from l'Arche that ends up turning into eighteen months. After a long period of following traces of my ancestry and of deeply moving experiences, I end up in a Trappist monastery, in Oka, sixty kilometers outside of Montreal. I decide to stay there for an extended retreat.

I get a taste of God's gentleness through the considerations of Father Lucien, a Cistercian with a broad, pastoral and luminous smile. We go on long, silent walks together. After three months, as we're wandering along, he says:

"Do you think you could be a Cistercian, or a Dominican?"

He knows how much affection I have for Father Thomas Philippe.

I look at him: "Father, I'll give you the answer tomorrow at noon. The Blessed Virgin will tell me."

Why did I say that? That's not like me.

The next day, a beautiful young woman named Sonia comes to see me:

"I have large house where I welcome handicapped people. I heard that you have some experience in the area and that you spent several months at Jean Vanier's l'Arche. Would you be willing to help me?"

As promised, I meet Father Lucien and say:

"Well, Father, the Blessed Virgin gave me an answer. I won't become a Cistercian or a Dominican. I'm going to go live with handicapped people."

He looks at me with his gentle smile, walks me to the car and gives me a blessing. As we're leaving Oka, I see him on the path waving goodbye with both hands. There's another priest who'll be in my heart forever. What an unbelievable treat from heaven!

For a year, I would live with Sonia and five handicapped residents of Sainte-Marthe, near Oka, on the lake, communing deeply with nature and with my wounded brothers. But one night I suddenly sense the need to return to France. The next day, I fly out of Montreal, toward Brussels. Eight hours later, I land in Belgium. I retrieve my backpack and start thumbing for a ride. Two cars later, I'm on the road toward the Farm at Trosly-Breuil. What a joy it is to get back to Father Thomas and the whole band the Good Lord gave me: Janine, Régine, aunt Agnès, Simone, Guy, Jean-Bernard, Dominique and the others. In my heart, they're family.

We celebrate. And yet, in the exuberance I sense an absence. Someone's missing. I know who it is. After the meal, I excuse myself and duck out:

"I have to go see a friend."

Janine, looking a little uneasy, stops me and says:

"Tim, your friend is in the hospital. She doesn't want to see anyone, she's letting herself die..."

In a heartbeat, I'm out the door and grabbing my bike out of the garage. It starts up without a fuss. I tear down to the hospital in Compiègne.

"You can't see her, sir, she's in ICU..."

"Well, that's just it ma'am, she needs me for the intensive care!" I gently push my way past the nurse and find my friend's room. The old woman is stretched out, white as a ghost, eyes closed and with hoses coming out of her every old which way. As I see her, my strength fails and sadness gets the better of me. I move closer and whisper in her ear:

"Your Canadian's back."

I place a gentle kiss on her withered cheek. She opens her eyes and smiles at me as if I'd come back from the dead.

"Aren't you a rascal? I crossed the ocean to see you and here you are in a hospital. You're going to get yourself out of here and get better, right?"

I can't stand hospitals. Too many bad memories, I gave enough already. I'm suddenly awkward and can't find the words. My friend runs her hand along my arm. In a mere whisper she tells me she loves me but that she wants to join her husband. This confession is too much for me to hear; her desire to leave on the Great Voyage. I love her and I don't want to share her with heaven, nor do I want to wait for eternal life to see her again. I give her another kiss and run out, away from this frightening white world.

I rage! I rail at God. As I'm bawling him out, I get hit by a car. I grab the driver through the window and shake him like a tree. The poor guy couldn't help it, I was walking in the middle of the road! The pain is overwhelming.

My return is a rude awakening. All my things have been stolen out of the attic at the Farm. Everything went, my dishes, my boxing gloves and especially the pictures of my father. Now that I'm nearly at peace with him in my heart, I can't even look at him anymore...

As if that weren't enough: my trainer took off with all my savings. He emptied my bank account.

I've got nothing left.

Every day for a month I go stand beside my old friend from Trosly. Every day I feel her slip away a little more. Every day she expresses her love for me, but I can't hold her back.

She dies with her hand in mine. That night, I cry in silence before her still body, this old woman from Trosly. My only consolation is knowing that her suffering has ended and that in the Good Lord's mansion she can once again be with the man she loved so much. This same thought that had made me so mad, I now find comforting.

Out in the street, my heart is unsettled, up and down. I ask God to give her a hardy welcome. At the same time, I tell him off for taking her away.

This woman had lived in Trosly for a long time. I had been warned when I arrived:

"Watch it, she's not very friendly and she doesn't like handicapped people."

One day, as a few of us are out wandering with some of the handicapped boys from the home, we pass by her yard. We all begin marveling at this flower garden that would put the finest reviews to shame. The birds are happy there and have taken to nesting by the dozens among the branches in a concert chirping and cooing. We stop and comment on its splendor. She's there tilling a strip of turf with a hoe when she spots us. Oh my! There she goes hurling a slew of invectives that would make a pirate blush. I look her straight in the eyes. She does the same, then goes back to turning the soil.

We finish our walk. I accompany the boys back to the home, grab a hoe and head back to her house. I walk into her yard and start digging at the other end of the walkway until she notices me.

"What are you doing here?" she asks. "I didn't say you could come in!"

"I'm here to help you, I like working the earth."

In no time I've got her strip tilled. She wants to pay me, I refuse.

"Why did you help me?"

"I wanted to... And a little while ago you came down on me like a storm. I wanted to bring you a rainbow. Now that the ground is tilled, we can start dreaming about vegetables and flowers!

She smiles and invites me to have some tea.

That's how we tamed each other. I came back often to have tea with her. Her heart opened up little by little. Her name was Mrs. Herman. Widowed about fifteen years earlier, she'd been living alone. In the village, some people had nicknamed her "the nazi." That hateful tag had hurt her terribly. That was why she was so defensive right off. In fact, her heart was more like her flower garden.

My departure for Canada had been a tremendous loss for her. She had written me long, affectionate, maternal letters. We had in common a love of beauty and some of the wounds in our souls.

In her hospital room, a short time before she died, I asked her:

"When you see God, tell him about me. Be my advocate. I've got a pretty long record to clear up. I want to change. Ask the Lord to help me become a just and loving man, and to find a good woman.

My messenger took flight.

She kept her word, beyond all my expectations.

Chapter 25

Age Twenty-Two
The Girl from the Home of Happiness

After Mrs. Herman's death, I'm itching to get on the road again. I head off to Rome to visit Mother Madeleine, then to see a British-Canadian girl in Florence. From there I make my way into Austria, to Salzburg, to see a German friend, a musician I knew in Trosly. She shares an apartment and her life with four other musicians. I fall in love with this women's orchestra and wind up spending five months with them in a large house they've rented in Salzburg. My muses are from five different countries, they each have distinct personalities and play a different instrument. The globe-trotter of differences has everything he could have hoped for.

They introduce me to classical music and show me a world of harmonies I had never known. These refined and educated ambassadors of beauty nourish me with culture and affection. One afternoon, although I've been living among them in perfect unison, and without knowing why, I have a sudden urge to return to Paris. Rather abruptly, I announce my departure to my five friends who, with a sad farewell, accompany me that same evening to the Salzburg train station.

At five o'clock the next morning, I see Lady Giraffe and her long neck. For breakfast I make my way over to Christelle's, a friend of mine living in Paris' 15th district.

"Someone name Martine is looking for you," she tells me. "Something about an apartment to fix up. Here's her phone number."

Martine is a friend from l'Arche, a simple girl in spite of her rather well-to-do family background. I call her.

"Hey, little brother, where are you? In Paris?"

"Since five this morning. Do you need me?"

"Yes, I'm fixing up my apartment near Trocadéro. I need a hand."

"Alright, I'm your man, I'm on my way."

An hour later, there I am at Vineuse Street. Fancy apartment building. I climb the stairs and ring the bell. Martine opens, looks at me and gives me a hug. I find her just the way she was, after months of being away: tall brunette, very direct.

"Hi, little brother. Thanks for coming so quickly."

She starts explaining her projects. We get to work. All day I'm painting, sawing, sanding, nailing, putting up shelves. By that evening, completely worn out, I sit down to take a breather. Martine tells me she's in love with me. Lucky for me I'm already sitting down and not likely to fall much further. Complete surprise!

I've known Martine for three years. For a year and a half I've been praying for her to meet a nice guy who'd be the love of her life. I never dared imagine, even for a hundredth of a nanosecond, that that guy might be me. I fall in love with just about every girl that goes by; not with her. She's from kind of a preppy crowd, comfortable with everyone and a good listener. People come to tell her their life story, ask her for advice.

She's tops just about any way you look at it. Pretty much out of reach for a guy like me. There's an abyss between us.

"No, Martine, it can't work between us. We're from different worlds. You're upper class, I'm a street kid. It's not a neighborhood we've got between us, it's a gulf."

She fights back, argues, pushes:

"Is it our differences that scare you? And you call yourself a globe-trotter of differences? Please. . ."

In spite of her arguments, and especially of her love, I keep resisting. I leave her thinking: "Don't fall in love, Tim, don't fall into the trap."

Only I've still got to finish the work on her apartment... I see Martine every day. Every day I fall in love a little more. "No, Tim, hold on, man, don't get carried away by the current..." I've got no more control over my feelings, I'm like a drunk pilot behind the controls of a plane gone haywire.

What am I supposed to do? I find her fascinating. Bubbly, joyful, artistic... Her voice is so beautiful. When she starts singing along with her guitar, I'm spellbound. The paint roller's moving on its own. I lay down four coats without even noticing. For Martine's beautiful eyes and through the grace of her voice, I could paint the Eiffel Tower!

After the fifth coat, Martine stops playing and I stop painting... To celebrate our accomplishment, she offers to take me to see her family in the area of Bordeaux.

A few hours later, she introduces me to her father, a British lord sort of fellow, somewhat of a jovial poet, amiable type. Her mother is a dignified, refined, queen mother type with a distinguished demeanor and impeccably neat hair. I'm impressed. There's also her oldest brother, Antoine—who could be a twin to King Juan Carlos—Evelyne, her older sister, a social worker—brings back memories—and her last brother, also older than Martine, whose look of distinguished young fighter I find particularly impressive. We have a hard time getting a handle on each other. Our home planets are in different galaxies.

Dinner is served. I watch them carefully during the meal: laughter, affection and kindness. I can't believe it. I'm getting the silverware all mixed up.

Coffee in the living room. It's the same routine. I'm bursting inside: "It's all a show, buddy. They're playing it up just to impress you!" An entire loving family just doesn't fit in my register. If their affection is genuine, I can't bear the thought of having missed out on it. If they're putting me on, the whole show is pitiful, hypocritical and mean. Either way, I can't stand it. I head outside for a breath of fresh air.

As I walk in the yard, the air calms my nerves, the blanket of night settles me down. I start thinking. Why would they fake it? What could they get from a masquerade?

I have to admit, I'm taken by the thoughtfulness of Martine's father. His broad knowledge and refinement remind me of Monsieur Léon. He's a man of the world, in the noble sense of the word. He knows how to listen to a guest and to value him, conveying his knowledge without overwhelming the person he's speaking to. He leads a conversation by calling on each participant to voice their opinion and to reach shared understanding. I'm amazed by this wise man. His intelligence is matched by his heart. He radiates a profound and fascinating inner harmony.

Martine's mother is more reserved. As with a precious stone, you have to look closely to discover all the hidden facets.

Come on, Tim, go back inside. Stop pouting. Look at all the differences, you like playing at that. I head back inside. I can tell Martine is relieved to see me relaxed and smiling. I decide to look on these people through eyes of love.

After the weekend in the country, the return trip is less than happy. It's not easy to hash things out over the loud sputtering of Martine's Beetle. She tells me that our many differences make for a rather delicate issue... I reply that that was my first objection to her declaration of love. What she told me then was that it didn't matter! Make up your mind, already!

I'm fuming and tell off the Good Lord while I'm at it: what does He want, really?

For the next ten days things remain muddled.

I keep screwing up. Love has made me dumb and awkward. The telephone doesn't help. Misunderstandings are piling up.

One morning I get up and say to God:

"I'm neither the type to commit suicide for love, nor the type to suffer for no reason. Right now, things are pretty lame and I'm not likely to keep this up much longer."

The next weekend we're off on a pilgrimage to Chartres to pray to the Virgin of Bel Amour. I clean out the flower shop at Montparnasse and lay an enormous bouquet, not at my beloved's feet but at those of the black Virgin. I pray with flowers and say to her:

"If you don't come up with a miracle, tomorrow I'm saying goodbye to Martine and going back home, to Canada."

The next evening, with my plane ticket in my pocket, I go knock on Martine's door. She greets me. Suddenly, an absolute certainty forcefully and mysteriously imposes itself upon us. God wants us to be together. It's just that clear and simple. Yes, God wants us together. Martine is free of all her questions and we decide to get engaged. Right then she says:

"Let's go to the final ten o'clock Mass Sacré-Cœur at Montmartre!"

I've got my answer. While she finishes getting herself ready, I'm looking to connect with my heavenly Father to thank him and to apologize. We hop in a taxi. I'm as proud as a peacock with such a wonderful fiancée by my side. It's bringing tears to my eyes. Now, arm in arm with a love I hadn't dared hope for, I walk these streets I so often wandered on foot, in despair. How beautiful Paris is on this night of May '78!

In the Church of Sacré-Cœur, we hold the most intimate of engagements. Martine and I and our two witnesses, God and the Virgin Mary.

Our differences push us to secrecy. How can we explain our love to Martine's family and to our friends? They'll think we're kidding.

For three months, nearly every Sunday, we undertake a Parisian pilgrimage. We pray that in their hearts Martine's parents might be ready to receive the bomb we're about to drop. We start our pilgrimage at Trocadéro Plaza, across from Lady Giraffe, praying the rosary on our way toward the chapel of the miraculous medallion, on Bac Street, then toward Notre Dame, before heading up toward Sacré-Cœur, at Montmartre, where we attend the evening Mass before going to celebrate our love over a good dish of couscous near Pigalle.

After three months of our secret engagement, we decide to announce our wedding day, only six weeks before the chosen date so as to keep them all from theorizing about our differences in pedigree. We're meeting my in-laws at their home in Arcachon. They don't yet suspect the good news we want to share with them.

Martine shows me a large white house near the pier. It's her grandmother's place, where she used to vacation as a child.

My throat tightens. I'm overwhelmed with emotion as a clear, intense memory has me transfixed. I can see myself on that pier, my weak body still fragile on legs that have just been fixed up, my head shaved, dreaming in front of that white house, while the nun's veils are flapping in the wind like cormorants' wings.

The large white house that Martine is showing me near the pier is the home of happiness of my childhood. I recognize it. I can see the miraculous medallion that one of the nice nuns gave me at the rehabilitation center. I remember the vow I made as a child: "Later, when I'm a man, I'll marry a girl from here."

Fifteen years later, the girl from the home of happiness is here, holding my hand. She was playing on this terrace while I was dreaming on the pier. She tells me that, in her heart, she always felt sorry for those orphans who had no family.

After a quiet dinner, Martine explains to her parents that we love each other and that we're going to get married.

Long silence.

My future father-in-law, a prayerful and generous man, exclaims:

"Aaaaah, what good news!"

He had often told his children that "marriage is hard enough without throwing differences in social background into the mix."

Nevertheless, he welcomes his future son-in-law with an extraordinarily open heart and mind.

Martine's mother is in shock, winded. She can't contain her emotion and, in words full of faith, says:

"It's amazing... Really... It's something we'll understand by living it."

For us, the effect of our prayers is palpable.

Chapter 26

Age Twenty-Three
The Wedding of the Prodigal Son

I'm off to a good start. The morning of our civil marriage, I'm late getting to the town hall. To look my best, I washed and braided my long hair and polished my Cossack boots until I could see the clouds going by in them like in a mirror. I lost track of the time... I tear off like a madman.

I arrive at the 16th district town hall, sweating up a storm, my hair still wet. Someone's going around asking everyone but me who the groom is. Finally I tap him on the shoulder and wearing my Easter Sunday smile I say:

"I'm the groom!"

He gets this fried marlin look on his face and I just stare right back at him. He regains his composure and gives me a solemn introduction. Everyone's dressed to the nines. Martine is stunning.

The yes I give to my commitment before this gathering is all the more solemn considering I shouldn't even be alive at this point in time.

Two weeks ago, I was riding my bike out onto La Motte Picquet Plaza when a Beetle burned a red light on Commerce Street. In a split second I realize there's no way for me to avoid the collision. I'm thinking: "I'm done for, I'm dead." My hand moves in spite of me, instinctively: I hit the gas. The bike lurches forward and hits. I'm airborne, flying over the top of the car, and roll to the ground on the other side. Wham! My leg has tripled in size and my eyebrow is bleeding. I'm not dead. I'm even good and alive and very relieved that my trip to heaven has been postponed. I have no desire to die...

For the reception, my friend Catherine has opened to us her heart and her beautiful apartment on Breteuil Avenue. A few years ago, I used to sleep in a bike hangar nearby...

Marc, Martine's witness, is rather impressed with my Cossack's boots. He checks out my street-level mirrors, looks me over not without some curiosity and, with a touch of envy, in a very 16th district tone, as if he were asking about a cocktail recipe, says:

"How do you manage to stay so... natural?"

Admittedly, we don't shop the same stores, all his shoes come from Weston's. As he's talking to me, Marc keeps flipping his hand and fiddling with his wrist, drawing my attention to his wrist. I ask him about it; he wanted nothing more:

"So, what's the matter with your watch, does it tickle?"

"This is no watch, my friend!"

"Well, it sure as heck looks like a watch! So, what is it?"

Marc is delighted and, having strutted around for a bit and built up the suspense, says:

"Ahem... It's a... ahem... A Rolex!"

"OK... And what does a Rolex have that a watch doesn't?"

"You're totally in the dark, buddy! A Rolex is like the Rolls Royce of watches! It's a Swiss gem with a mechanism assembled entirely by hand. It'll never wear out, it's got a lifetime guarantee and runs a couple grand..."

"Well, I'll bet you I can stop your indestructible, lifetime-guaranteed Rolex just by putting it on my wrist."

"You don't know what you're talking about, man, you can't stop a Rolex!"

"Not a single watch works on me!"

"Fine, but a Rolex is a Rolex! I'll take your bet..."

I strap his Rolex into my wrist. Tick, tick. Five minutes go by. I'm starting to have doubts about the magnetism that usually wrecks any watch I try and put on. Tick, tick. The Rolex is unshakeable, and Marc is triumphant. Tick, tick. Just as he starts crying victory, the second hand begins slowing down... He grows pale.

"No, don't tell me... My Rolex..."

A minute later, the Rolex is dead. Marc is livid. He looks at me, the Big-Chief-who-stops-Rolexes.

"Don't worry, it's got a lifetime guarantee!"

Marc is my exact opposite. We'll get to be friends—thank you, Rolex—and synchronize our watches. The more I get to know him, the more aware I become of the suffering in what are considered "good families." Nothing but wounds, hidden under the outer signs of wealth! Divorced parents, twenty years of therapy, the security of a bank account and an incurably sad heart... Thanks to Marc, I discover that poverty is not simply a material issue, and that people suffer more intensely and less visibly from emotional and spiritual misery.

The day after our civil marriage, we have our wedding before God, in the church at Trosly, surrounded by our friends from l'Arche. Their hearts are like a flurry of Sundays. The feast is magnificent. Everyone comes by to congratulate me:

"You sure are lucky to have a woman like her!"

No argument. Though I wouldn't mind hearing that my wife is also lucky to have a husband like me!

The Gospel for wedding Mass was written especially for me. This page, written by Saint Luke two thousand years ago, seems completely new to me. It's the story of a son who gets into it with his dad, leaves home and then years later comes back to his father...

"...And he arose and came to his father. But while he was yet at a distance, his father saw him and had compassion, and ran and embraced him and kissed him. And the son said to him,

'Father, I have sinned against heaven and before you; I am no longer worthy to be called your son.'

But the father said to his servants:

'Bring quickly the best robe, and put it on him… and let us eat and make merry; for this my son was dead, and is alive again; he was lost and is found…'"

The Word of God is alive. It gives me ideas…

"Philippe, do you take Martine to be your wife?"

Here we are. The fateful moment. An "I do" is three letters, two syllables to pronounce, a half second for a lifelong commitment.

I do means I do for life.

"I do."

At that moment, with those words, it's all been decided. I swear to show up my genetic heritage, with the help of the Holy Spirit and our love.

Then it's time for us to celebrate!

In marriage, after having tested it during our engagement, Martine and I continue to explore the abyss of our differences. I'm more like a planer; Martine's more like sandpaper. We love each other and, inevitably, make each other suffer. Martine lives with her heart and her front door wide open. She welcomes everyone at any time, while I have an obsessive need for privacy. She bakes me cakes—I've developed a thing for good food—and as thanks I say:

"I need affection more than I need sweets."

Abrupt and coarse, I often wound her with my words, sharp as knives, and my quick temper.

Being different means having to adapt to the other person, getting to know their owner's manual, allowing oneself to be known and always compromising. Adopting one another takes lots of time, patience and gentleness.

I suffer especially when Martine's family gets together. I feel excluded from their connection. We don't have any common ground. Sure, I understand that they'd have a hard time integrating a bit of a head case without a family, with Cossack boots and hair half way to his waist, but what I don't accept is feeling like I haven't been adopted. I can't stand family gatherings. I don't feel like a son, even when my father-in-law says, on the day we make our love known: "You're like a son to me!"

The hardest part is always being "like," and never actually just being. It's nothing anyone can help.

Family reunions tear me apart. I get paralyzed by fears: fear of being uninteresting, of being different, of seeming uneducated... I turn into a wounded beast. I overreact.

"You never have to make any effort," I tell Martine. "You've never been to your in-laws.' And with good reason!"

I'm suffocating in Paris, pacing like a caged lion. I miss my friends the trees and a few animals to tame. We get a few offers of rural worksites to take over in the Landes area or in Brittany. What does my Pal the Good Lord think about all this? Where does he want us? The day after I ask Him the question, Marie-Hélène Mathieu, the head of the Christian Office for the Handicapped where Martine works, asks my wife:

"Would you be willing to care for our branch in Lourdes? The woman in charge there has to quit for health reasons."

Here's my Pal's answer.

It's decided, we're leaving for Lourdes.

A short time before our move, my wife takes me to a welcome center in Châteauneuf-de-Galaure, in the Drôme region, to attend a retreat. Big compromise. I go out of love for my wife because I can't picture myself sitting for six days listening to a priest. Even if the preacher is none other than Father Thomas Philippe's brother. His name is Marie-Dominique—weird name for a guy—and wears the same white Dominican's robe—what is it, some kind of family illness or something? He's no bigger than his brother. His eyes shine behind lenses as thick as a magnifying glass. Everyone calls him Marie-Do. The theme of the retreat: the Apocalypse, the last book of the Bible. The name reminds me more of Calypso; that's a night club.

When Marie-Do begins the retreat, silence settles in. It would remain for six days. His talks are enthralling. Thoroughly captivated, I take everything down in a notebook.

With everyone basking in the light, six days go by without a word. They look kindly on one another. An unexplainable closeness emerges without exchanging a single word.

In the middle of the week, the retreatants who wish to do so are offered the opportunity to visit Marthe Robin. She's a simple peasant woman from the area who lives Christ's Passion in her body, they say, and who radiates goodness and truth. That's hard to believe for a great sinner of limited intellect. She lives cloistered in a room on the farm where she was born, keeping the shutters closed because her wounded eyes can't stand the light anymore. People come from all over the world to entrust her with their prayer intentions and to receive advice.

People wait a long time to see her and the list of candidates is already long. Martine wants to sign up, while I, the macho, proud type, say: "Don't need it!"

During lunch, a young woman takes the microphone and announces the first seven people called to see Marthe Robin that very afternoon. To my utter amazement, we're the first ones called. I look at Martine and can't help saying:

"But, we didn't even sign up!..."

The eyes of two hundred retreatants turn toward us. I turn beet red.

I have no choice, I follow my wife. We make our way up to the Robin farm, up on a plateau. A rustic kitchen with a wood stove has been turned into a waiting room. People are speaking in whispers. A young girl leads Martine and me into a dark room. It seems very mysterious. We sit down near a bed barely discernable in the darkness. I imagine that this holy woman will immediately see into my soul and chase me away with a resounding "Out, Satan!" No, it's a clear, surprisingly young voice emerging from the shadows to welcome us. We tell this invisible woman that we're newlyweds and very, very different from one another. She laughs!

She laughs and says:

"For the Good Lord, that amounts to nothing. Your relationship must be based on Faith, Hope and Love."

Martine tells her we're expecting a child. She rejoices and marvels. She speaks of children as if she had raised them her entire life.

I tell her about my fears of becoming a father, considering my less-than-encouraging background, and about my dread of recreating the wounds I received. She listens then answers:

"Your children will grow to the measure of your love."

These words become inscribed within me with letters of fire.

As we're explaining our plans to move to Lourdes and to find a house, she stops us:

"A house to welcome those whom the Blessed Virgin will send you!"

Martine and I look at each other. Ever since our engagement, we've dreamt of a home we could share. Without knowing us, Marthe gives us confirmation and reassures us, saying:

"The Blessed Virgin will show you."

By the end of our meeting, in spite of the darkness, we can now make out this little body, curled up under a sheet, whose voice is as soft as an angel's and whose words are light.

Having made our way back out to the courtyard of this farm, we're blinded and astounded by what we have just experienced. This simple moment, of such importance in our existence, is a real cornerstone. Here we are, full of hope, thrilled. Marthe Robin would forever hold a place of utmost importance in our life.

At the end of the retreat, one of the accompanying priests asks me to tell my story. I'm reluctant, I don't want to. Ultimately, I obey. After that day I entered a period of silence that was to last eleven years, until my father's death.

Chapter 27

Age Twenty-Four
At Lourdes, in Mary's Hands

Lourdes…

As a kid, that word would feed my dreams, like Canary Islands or Seychelles. It made me think of huge mountains, torrential waters, fresh air, wild forests and freedom…

One day when I was little, the Mayor of our village had given each of the kids a five franc coin. I had bet the whole fortune at once in a raffle at the town's festival. The first prize was a trip to Lourdes. I was sure I was going to take it all—I wanted it too badly for it not to come true… My disappointment was as great as my illusion had been. I had lost everything at once: my coin and my dream. The richest boy in town had won the trip to Lourdes.

I remember the story this evening as we're moving in. Along the little road snaking past the churchyard, the beam from my truck's headlights had caught the sign: "Lourdes." It's two-thirty in the morning and a myriad candles are still burning in the night on the other side of the Gave, in front of the cave where Mary appeared to Bernadette, the shepherd girl. God's got some memory! He doesn't just give me a trip but a whole life in Lourdes. My Pal always grants more than expected.

We live in an apartment on Grotte Street, with a view of the castle. I feel hemmed in by these four walls. I'm looking for some old ruin to fix up in the neighboring countryside. Every evening I say to Martine:

"Come take a look, I think I found it."

Every evening, she follows me quietly. We look around, then drop the idea. That's not it.

It's become all the more urgent now that we're sharing our home with Roger, a boy originally from Senegal. He celebrated Christmas with us this winter. Two months earlier, a judge and a social worker contacted us with the news that Roger had nearly died of a drug overdose and that in the hospital he had said:

"There's only one way for me to make it, that's to go to my brother Tim's, in Lourdes."

The social worker asked us if we were willing to take him in...

"We'll take him! Send him down!"

That got me in trouble; serves me right. I didn't ask Martine's opinion. She doesn't wait to give it to me:

"We've got a baby and only two small rooms. Don't you think we're cramped enough as is?"

"Églantine will sleep in our room! Where's the problem? Martine, if we don't take Roger in, I won't go to church anymore. One day the Good Lord will say to me: 'I wanted to enter your home and you didn't welcome me...'"

Martine, the queen of open doors, accepted. She said yes in an act of faith. My hat's off to her.

Living God isn't always easy. Neither is living with Tim Guénard. And so, Roger arrives. He's a piece of walking entertainment. Addicted to heroine, two meters tall, he trundles his enormous frame around with a boom-box blaring on his shoulder. Fits of withdrawal follow fits of nervousness which follow bouts of depression. Life together is rather chaotic.

Roger's father was from Senegal, his mother from Normandy. They died in a car wreck along with his little sister. Left alone, Roger also experienced the wounds of abandonment and rejection. For his father's family, he wasn't black enough; for his mother's family, he wasn't white enough. The great singer, Josephine Baker adopted him. When she died, Roger's heart was shattered once again. Edith Piaf, his godmother, tried to get him a position as bellboy in some of the great Parisian palaces, but he would empty the champagne bottles in the hallways instead of serving the customers. Then, Roger the Black met heroin the "white," and his descent into hell...

Martine and I pray fervently to the Blessed Virgin to find us a spacious and open home. It's pretty urgent. We're starting to lose it. One day a real estate agent leads us over dirt paths, a few kilometers outside of Lourdes, to a large structure built into the side of a hill. It's love at first sight. It's an old farm that's been turned into a vacation home known as the Chalet Notre-Dame. What a wonderful treat my Pal has given us! "The Blessed Virgin will show you," Marthe Robin had told us...

We close the deal and immediately rededicate our future home: Notre-Dame Farm, to commemorate Father Thomas Philippe's farm and Marthe Robin's farm as well as the Virgin Mary's "signature."

There's a lot of work to be done. I'm not worried. We work on the Farm during the day, in the great outdoors, on our hill. Roger just keeps cranking up love songs from Julio Iglesias. "Qué amore..." It gets old after a while, but not nearly as much as his games:

"What will you give me if I stay clean for a week?"

"Nothing, Roger, nothing. You're quitting drugs for yourself, not for me."

"Sure, that's what I figured, Tim, you don't love me, I'm going to kill myself."

When he first arrived, I didn't feel at all secure. When I'd wake up in the morning, I'd run and check to see if he was still alive. Then I got used to it and I let him play his games.

One day, I don't know why, but Roger didn't bring his boombox to the Farm. No love songs, no Julio Iglesias? How nice to have a bit of a break, some silence. Finally! As I'm painting the front of the house, he shows up, climbs the ladder and gives me a hug: "Tim, my brother, I love you. I feel good here. Did you notice how beautiful it all is, the silence, the birds... Hey, Tim, would you like some coffee?"

"Yeah, sure. You know what, Roger? I like the silence too, and I'm glad to see you appreciate it..."

You could have knocked me over, I can't believe it! I'm so grateful for the sudden change. Alright, I keep painting with a light heart, giving thanks. A half hour goes by. He's taking a while to get his coffee ready. Finally, Roger shows up. He's trying to walk carefully, stumbling along. His black skin has turned jaundiced. I rub my eyes, thinking the stark white of the paint has done something to my vision. He splutters:

"Here, br...bro, the cof...coffee's r...ready!"

"Thanks Roger. Hey, are you alright? You look a little funny!"

"Yeaaaah... I'm alright... I'm alright..."

He turns around and lands spread eagle in the mud, completely wrecked. He got himself high on a cocktail of medicine and alcohol. It's painful to see his enormous body so torn up by the abuse. I get him back on his feet and say:

"Roger, we're going to head back to the apartment right away. Don't move, I'm going to get the car!"

As I'm walking toward my truck, I hear a loud noise. While I had my back turned, Roger managed to start his moped and is taking off down hill. Oh my God! He's about to take the first turn at full speed... Crap! He's going straight, he's going over the edge. He's launching, it's a death jump! I'm cursing myself for having left him even a moment alone. I run to the edge of the cliff, expecting to find a dead body at the bottom to the ravine. No, Roger's fall was broken by a bush. The moped is balancing on top of him. I have no idea how the whole thing is holding up! You'd think we were in a cartoon. Holding on to some small trees, I pull the bike back up, then go and get him. He's laughing his head off. Not me. I'm fed up.

No sooner is Roger back on his feet than he hops back on his moped and takes off, laughing all the more and, naturally, without my approval. For the second time a furious rage takes hold of me. All I can do is follow him, railing and reciting "Ave Marias" with a few improvisations tacked on:

"Mary, please protect this lunatic. Keep Roger alive. Don't let this be the hour of his death."

After five kilometers of zigzags that fortunately corresponded more or less to the turns in the road, we make it safely to the outskirts of Lourdes. Roger heads straight for the sign indicating "Lourdes," as if he wanted to reach some imaginary finish line. The moped tears underneath and crashes into a ditch, while Roger remains hanging from the sign. I just explode:

"Get in the car! I'm sick of this!"

He screams:

"My moped, my moped, I don't want to leave my moped!"

"Shut up, Roger! You'll get it tomorrow!"

I get him into the truck and we head home together.

On arriving at Grotte Street, he climbs the stairs to the apartment, heads into the bathroom and stays there for two hours.

"What's the matter with Roger?" asks Martine, "Has he been up to his old tricks again?"

I tell her the afternoon's adventures. It's come at a bad time, we're having a guest that evening. At the table Roger just stares at out friend like a zombie and keeps asking her name.

"What's your name? What's your name? Hey, what's your name?"

He's got us totally on edge. He goes back to the bathroom, but it doesn't get any better. He turns on Julio Iglesias.

While Martine and our friend are putting Églantine to bed, I snap. I run to the bathroom, grab the mirror, return to the living room and hold it right in front of him:

"Look at yourself!"

"No, no, I don't want to, leave me alone."

I stick the mirror right in his face:

"Look at yourself, damn it, look at yourself right in the eyes!"

"No, no, you can't make me do this, I don't want to see myself..."

I can't stand this guy anymore. I'm losing it. I go back to the bathroom, mirror in hand. Sitting there on the edge of the tub, I start bawling like a kid. He emptied me out. Not only is he aggravating but he won't leave me alone for a second! He pushes the door open. I'm thinking I'm going to tear this guy's head off, that I was a complete idiot to have wanted to welcome this kind of wacko, that you'll never catch me at it again; it's just more than I can handle. As I'm getting up to knock his block off, he puts his arms around me and in a pasty voice says:

"Tim, you're the only one who loves me, and I love you."

Silence.

I feel as if I were hearing a message that wasn't meant for me. For months, Roger kept threatening to commit suicide saying: "You don't love me," "What'll you give me if I don't shoot up?" "You don't care about me anyway," etc. Now he's comforting me with a declaration of love and tearful kisses.

Suddenly, he adds:

"Come on, brother, let's go see her!"

He gets up and tears out of the house like a whirlwind.

I know exactly what woman Roger wants to go see. It's his last chance. He fell in love with the Crowned Virgin of the church in Lourdes ever since I brought him, utterly discouraged, to sit at her feet the very night of his arrival. I was already fed up then. He had been screwing up time after time, all day long. I was about to snap.

From nine pm until one in the morning, we kept wandering back and forth between the statue of the Virgin and the apartment on Grotte Street; a kind of succession of mini pilgrimages interspersed with moments of crisis. From within, I couldn't stop looking up to heaven with silent, desperate cries for help:

"Mary, I can't take it anymore, this guy's running me ragged, he's getting on my nerves, sucking me dry, emptying me out... He's your child. I'll never be able to hold on, Martine was right. A man should always listen to his wife! Mary, you're my last hope. Don't abandon me, don't abandon Roger!

Unbelievable but true, at one in the morning, Roger had knelt in front of the statue. He was converted.

Ever since that memorable night, he often returned there alone. He would kneel in front of his beloved statue, raise his tremendous arms toward the heavens and, in the midst of a crowd, without the slightest human concern, would cry out:

"I love you, Mary, I'm going to take you away with me! Oh, I love you!"

He would return from his Marian cleansing washed, purified and at peace. Prayer seemed to be the best remedy for him during his bouts of withdrawal.

The day after our wild adventure, on this eleventh day of February, we're celebrating the feast of Our Lady of Lourdes. We're on our way back to the church with Martine and our little Églantine, just a few months old. There's a large crowd for the great procession. Roger takes the lead and starts parting the crowd, crying out:

"Come, my brother and sister, come, follow me!"

The bearers were there surrounding the cave where the bishop was praying in silence. Not the slightest bit intimidated, Roger calls out in his African accent:

"I want to see the bishop right away or I'll cause a scandal."

The bearers try to keep him quiet, without any luck.

"I want to see the bishop. Right away. It's very important..."

Intrigued by the ruckus, the bishop comes over, unafraid. Roger takes him by the hand. Without a word, the giant kisses the Episcopal ring with the devotion due to a relic.

He returns home overwhelmed by the encounter. Whatever happened within him? He would be forever changed. I believe that on that day, Roger was healed of many inner wounds, thanks to the Crowned Virgin and to this gesture from the bishop who came to him.

Roger stayed with us for a year and a half, then left for Montélimar. He would phone us from time to time from a bistro: "Hey brother. How's the Mama doing? Is she getting flowers? What about the bishop, is he doing well? Tell them I love them." His heart couldn't take the suffering anymore. The drugs had ravaged his body. Roger died not long after that. He went to be with his Mother in Heaven who took him in her arms and carried him up into the burning heart of God.

Roger, my brother, was the first of those "sent" to us.

Today, I am a happy man. That isn't what I thought yesterday. I give thanks for my past. It has given me this present, this unexpected gentleness.

Martine and I have four children. Water has flowed over the rocky bed of the Gave River. I've hung up my boxing gloves to take up beekeeping. It's more peaceful.

My new arena is my heart. The struggle for love takes place within each one of us, at every moment.

I've met thousands of young people, in schools, in prisons, in stadiums...

I tell them my favorite parable, the one that life taught me: the prayer of the manure pile.

To get beautiful flowers to grow in a garden, you need manure.

That's our past. God uses it to make us grow.

Manure straight from the horse's butt is too hot, to acidic and too heavy. It stinks and it's disgusting. If you spread it directly on flowers and seedlings, it burns them and crushes them.

You have to let manure sit for a while, dry out and decompose slowly. In time, it becomes malleable, odorless, light and fertile. Then it produces the most beautiful flowers and the most beautiful shrubs.

God uses our past like fertilizer for our lives. To make us grow. If you keep your head in the past, all steamed up, it'll choke you. You have to let it settle.

With the work of time and grace, all that is evil within us begins imperceptibly to disintegrate.

We must love what we were once ashamed of and which seemed reprehensible to us. The pile of manure will become fertile ground.

Our past, our suffering, our hardships and our cries are a hymn in the language of the poor.

We can't be today without having been yesterday.

No matter who you are, whatever harm you have suffered and however painful a past you have had, never forget, in your wounded memory, that an eternity of love awaits you.

Chapter 28

Seventy-Seven Times Seven

I nearly killed my father. Accidentally.

It happened back when I was first encountering God.

Fr. Thomas Philippe had started administering his forgiveness IV and I was feeling weird all over. I hadn't given up fighting yet.

One Saturday night, when my gang and I were scouring the countryside, we decided to round out our evening at an area night club. As soon as I was inside and my eyes got used to the light, I recognized two of my step-brothers in a corner of the bar. Given my not-so-pleasant memories, I decided to take off. Just as I was heading out, one of my buddies started a fight without even wanting to. The brawl quickly degenerated. Everybody joined in, my guys against everyone else in the place. Fists were flying everywhere.

In the shadows, I wasn't too sure who I was beating up on. I was landing my blows, my opponent was backing up. The other gang hopped in their cars and bolted. Seeing them leave, I started feeling an indescribable unease. I didn't sleep well that night.

Then next morning, I figured it out. It was my father I was beating up. He didn't defend himself. The guy I had just beaten the crap out of was the father I had dreamt of killing and hadn't seen in years. I felt awful.

Just a few months earlier, I would have been ecstatic. I found myself rejecting the moment of revenge I had wanted for so long.

The desire to forgive him came a while later, thanks to Frédéric's gift. His five typewritten lines opened my heart. They made me want to start my whole life from scratch. A life built on love, not on hate.

It was thanks to Frédéric's gift and to the words spoken by a little girl. Sylvie was six years old then. I met her while Social Services were trying to find her a home. Her father was a severe alcoholic and used to beat her. But she didn't want to leave him, she had put her hope in him and had hopes for him. One day she said to me:

"I want to stay with my papa. He's nice when he's not drunk."

I was touched by those words. Two years later, the man quit drinking. His daughter's hope saved him.

Thanks to Sylvie and Frédéric I started looking for the good in my father. I found some. I realized it was thanks to him that I had become a boxing champion. I owe him a part of the happiness I have today.

One day, in town, I came across a pretty young woman walking with a boy. I was taken aback as I recognized my step-sister and her brother. She had never been mean to me when we were kids, so I decided to go up to her. My nerves in a ball, I stepped right in front of her and asked:

"Do you know who I am?"

She thought for a moment then, turning suddenly toward her brother, said:

"I recognize him, he's daddy's son."

I was moved by the deeply affectionate way she said daddy. If she could speak of this man with such love, he couldn't possibly be bad. He must even have been an excellent father to his second children.

I learned, incidentally, that he sometimes washed my diapers by hand when I was little. My father used to beat me, but he washed my diapers!

So I went back to my father's house. Just like in the parable in the Gospel. He was living in a small house in the northern suburbs of Paris. I rang the doorbell. He opened. I recognized him in spite of all the time that had passed. His tall figure wasn't hunched over yet. He looked at me in silence, showing no surprise. He didn't say anything like "Oh, it's you, after all these years," or "Get the hell out of here, I never could stand you!" or even "My dear child, forgive me." No, he didn't say anything.

His eyes spoke for him.

I got right to the point, probably to handle my nerves:

"I've become a Christian, I forgive you. We can start our life over from scratch!"

That was the stupidest thing I ever did.

Right away, I could feel him stiffen. His eyes grew cloudy and darkened. He bent over as if he'd just been hit in the stomach.

I had just sent this man back into the hell of his past that he was trying so desperately to flee. All I had been was an egotistical bastard who, when it came down to it, had thought of only one thing: my own relief. To live this forgiveness for myself and myself alone. To give myself a brand new, clear conscience.

My father wasn't so lucky as to have a wife like mine and friends like the ones I had received. I often asked myself: why? Why did I have that chance and not him? No doubt he was trying to escape the grip of his guilt and the awful memories of his shame. He had tried to fix what he could by being a good father to his other children. He still couldn't forgive himself. He judged himself most harshly.

Then I came to him, after so many years apart, and threw my forgiveness in his face like a judgment and a condemnation.

Sometimes our hearts can offer a forgiveness our lips shouldn't express.

In the Gospel, when Christ addresses the adulterous woman that the Pharisees want to stone, he doesn't say: "I forgive you your nights of sin." He says nothing. He draws in the sand.

I left quickly, feeling guilty. I tried to fill the space between us by sending him postcards. Seems kind of stupid, doesn't it, postcards? Short notes telling him about my love of life, a knowing wink here and there, a happy moment I'd share with him on the fly.

After a few years, there was more present than past between us.

That's when I knew he could accept my forgiveness.

One day I learned he had stopped drinking. For someone so ill, that was an act of heroism. I found myself admiring him.

I learned of my father's death by chance. In 1990.

In the street, I came across an uncle and his son. The man recognized me and came up to me:

"Hey Tim, you must be happy."

"Happy...sure. Why?"

"You know your bastard father died?"

The wind was knocked out of me. My breath cut off. Silence. Anguish.

"...No...When?"

"Barely three months ago."

The cousin was nice. He knew what my father had put me through. He added:

"Ah, that bastard..."

I didn't hold it against my cousin. He didn't know that God had come into my life and turned it all inside out. But I was mad at God for taking my father from me so suddenly.

He took my father, my grandfather, my father-in-law and my Father Thomas. All of them died in a short period. That's a lot to handle. God worked on me in bulk.

Two years earlier, on the morning of my birthday, the phone rang at the house. Another uncle, on my mother's side, said:

"I have to see you, I need to talk to you... Something important... I'd rather we met alone, in private..."

We set a meeting in Lourdes a little while later. Come the time, I head into town. I find him with his wife.

"Your grandfather had to have his only remaining leg amputated..."

I can't believe it. He adds:

"Gangrene set in, the doctors couldn't do anything... he died."

I tried not to show my feelings, but the pain of never seeing that beloved grandfather again in this world tore a moan from my lips.

My uncle turned to his wife, saying:

"You see, I told you it would mean something to him..."

I turned my back on them, headed back up the mountain and cried a long while, running my hand over trees on the way.

I reached the Farm overwhelmed. Martine asked:

"Would you rather we put your birthday dinner off until tomorrow?"

"No, it's all part of life. I love you. We're going to celebrate."

That afternoon, I went back into town to get presents for everyone. I removed the sting of hatred that leads to hatred that leads to hatred... The vicious cycle has to be broken at any cost.

My birthday celebration lasted late into the night. I turned that hateful moment into happiness for others.

My Father Thomas died on February 4, 1993. He was eighty-seven years old. He died the way he had lived. He lived what he had preached. He became poor and small—he had so often taught the special presence of God within those who suffer and live in anguish.

Two years earlier he had had to leave his beloved Arche. He could no longer contain the flow of those who rushed to the Farm to receive his counsel, to have confession and to taste the love of the Lord through his compassion. When I found out that my good Father Thomas had returned to his Lord, I cried once again.

"The blessing of tears makes us small, it softens our hearts taking away everything hard and closed up," he would say. "The

Good Lord loves silence in front of others, but he also wants us to let our tears flow near Him, like little children…"

Forgiveness isn't a magic wand.

There's the forgiveness of will, then there's that of ability: we want to forgive but we can't. When we're finally able to, when our head and our heart finally agree, memories remain, painful things resurface, troubling our minds and rekindling hatred. This is the forgiveness of memory. It's not the easiest thing. It takes a lot of time.

For ten years, every morning, I would ask Martine: "Do you love me?" I couldn't bring myself to believe in her love. My healing happened over a long period. Yes, it takes time. I was fortunate to meet genuine people. They loved me with the seal of my past, they dared to accept my differences, the small steps of my wounded self. They listened to my suffering and kept loving me after the storms had passed. Now I have memories of having received.

The past can be awakened by a sound, a word, a smell, a noise, a gesture or a glimpse of a place… It takes next to nothing for the memories to come back. They jostle and claw at me. They remind me how sensitive I still am. I still hurt. I may never be completely at peace. I'll most likely have to start my forgiveness over, again and again. Is that the "seventy-seven times seven" that Jesus talks about?

Forgiving doesn't mean forgetting. It means accepting to live in peace with the offense. It's difficult when the wound has touched an entire body, marking it like a branding of death. I recently had to have my legs operated on: the blows I received from my father caused irreparable physical damage. The pain returns often, and with it, the memories.

In order to forgive, you have to remember. You can't hide the wound or bury it; on the contrary, you have to bring it to the light. A hidden wound gets infected and festers. It has to be looked at and listened to in order to become a source of life.

My witness is that there are no wounds that can't be slowly healed through love.

Until I was sixteen, I had wild dreams of my mother coming to take me back. Then I accepted the intolerable notion of having been abandoned by the woman who bore me. At that time I decided it would be better if I never saw her again.

And yet, it happened. By surprise. It was after my wedding. An aunt had invited me to a family reunion without telling me I would see my mother there. I suddenly found myself in front of a brown-haired woman, young and attractive.

She didn't make a move when she saw me. No expression.

I went up to her and said:

"My one and only dream is to have a kiss from you..."

She drew back imperceptibly.

"...or your hand on my shoulder, if you want. Just one gesture. That'll be enough..."

She kept her distance and answered:

"You're just like your father... honor, nothing but honor!"

I waited for a few seconds for a gesture that couldn't come. I headed for the door. I was on my way out when my mother caught up to me on the stoop. She asked:

"Have you forgiven your father?"

"Yes, I forgave him."

She closed up. Her face hardened. Most likely she couldn't accept the fact that I had forgiven this man who had broken me physically. She couldn't take the idea that I could put both of them on the same level of forgiveness. She said:

"Yes, you're just like your father. You'll be a bad husband and a bad father..."

Some words carry more violence than fists. Words issued from the poison of despair, of powerlessness. My mother didn't know the weight of her words.

It took another woman, Martine, my wife, to purge me of that mortal venom. She cared for me with an angelic patience, day after day.

Thanks to Martine, today I can say something unimaginable: the joy I get from our four children, I owe also to my mother. She gave me life, that immeasurable treasure.

Today, I struggle to be a good father, a good husband and a good son…to God the Father.

My children have become my roots. With them, the wounded man that I am has received many healings. When they call me papa, I get a wonderful chill running down my spine. An exquisite feeling. It's the most beautiful thing in the world. I remember all the times I missed out on "my papa." I give thanks. And I entrust into the hands of God the Father all those children who have no one to call "my papa."